For Future Generations

For Future Generations

RECONCILING GITX̲SAN AND CANADIAN LAW

P. Dawn Mills

PURICH
PUBLISHING
LIMITED
SASKATOON, SK. CANADA

Purich Publishing Ltd.
Box 23032, Market Mall Post Office, Saskatoon, SK, Canada, S7J 5H3
Phone: (306) 373-5311 Fax: (306) 373-5315 Email: purich@sasktel.net
Website: www.purichpublishing.com

Library and Archives Canada Cataloguing in Publication

Mills, Patricia Dawn, 1954-
For future generations : reconciling Gitsan and Canadian law / Patricia Dawn Mills.

(Purich's aboriginal issues series)
Includes bibliographical references and index.
ISBN 978-1-895830-34-7

1. Gitksan Indians – Legal status, laws, etc. – British Columbia. 2. Gitksan Indians – Legal status, laws, etc. – Canada. 3. Gitksan Indians – Claims. 4. Gitksan Indians – Land tenure. 5. Gitksan Indians – Politics and government. 6. Gitksan Indians – Government relations. I. Title. II. Series.

E99.K55M45 2008   346.71104′32089972   C2008-901355-7

Edited, designed, and typeset by Donald Ward, who also created the map.
Cover design by Duncan Campbell.
Cover art: "It's Time to Wear Our Blankets," by Art Wilson, 'Wii Muk'wilixw, of the Laxgibuu of Anspayaxw.
Photograph of cover art by Bob Michayluik Photography.
Index by Ursula Acton.
Printed and bound in Canada.

Purich Publishing gratefully acknowledges the assistance of the Government of Canada, through the Book Publishing Industry Development Program, and the Government of Saskatchewan, through the Cultural Industries Development Fund, for its publishing program. The publisher also acknowledges the University of Saskatchewan Native Law Centre for providing maps for study and possible inclusion.

This book is printed on 100 per cent post-consumer, recycled, and ancient-forest-friendly paper.

This book is dedicated to the Gitxsan people, as well as the researchers, support staff, lawyers, jurists, and their families associated with *Delgam'Uukw (Muldoe) et al.* v. *R. in Right of British Columbia and Attorney General of Canada,* 1991, 1993 *and* 1997.

❧

I wish also to acknowledge my family and friends, in all that I have undertaken, for their support and unconditional love.

❧

The Gitxsan words used in this book are from the Western Gitxsan dialect. Art Wilson, *'Wii Muk'wilixw,* of the *Laxgibuu* of *Anspayaxw,* reviewed the glossary for accuracy. The author gratefully acknowledges his work; any mistakes or variances are those of the author.

Contents

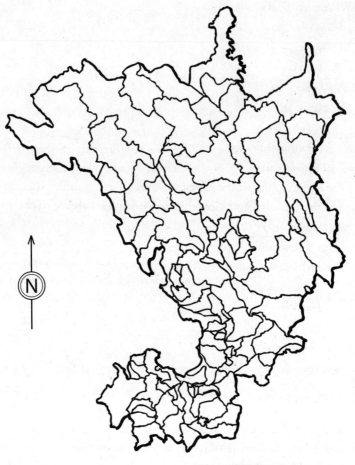

*Gitxsan Traditional Territory
showing internal wilp boundaries.*

Foreword

THIS BOOK IS ABOUT THE GIT̲XSAN AND THEIR CONTINUING STRUGGLE TO convince the Crown that their first responsibility, as a people, lies in protecting the land and all that lives from it; and that the *Simgigyet* and *Sigidim haanak'a* (hereditary chiefs) are obligated to ensure that all their *wilp* members (house members) will have sufficient food and other resources for future generations. This has been and remains the motivation of the Git̲xsan to reconcile their title and rights with that of the Crown according to the *Ayooks* of *Naa hlimoot'* (laws of sharing).

I have known Patricia Dawn Mills for the better part of twenty years. We met during the original trial of *Delgam'Uukw* in 1987. Dawn has proved to be a good observer who comprehends well what the Git̲xsan seek to achieve in the negotiated reconciliation of their Aboriginal title and their right to self-government based on the *Gim litxwid* (the alliance of *Simgigyet* and *Sigidim haanak'a*), as well as their legal challenge to British Columbia's claim of ownership and the province's right to unilaterally extinguish Aboriginal rights. Dawn's work seeks to give conceptual and practical meaning to the reconciliation paradigm articulated by the Supreme Court of Canada for the resolution of disputes involving Aboriginal right and title to First Nations' traditional territory. A resolution of these conflicts has not yet been achieved, either through the existing British Columbia treaty process or through the environmental impact assessment process. Litigation is not designed to provide detailed working models for reconciliation agreements, nor can it reasonably be expected to.

In 1995, Dawn Mills was asked to write a position paper for the A. C. Hamilton inquiry, "A New Partnership," in support of our argument for the inclusion of Git̲xsan *ayooks* as a framework for treaty negotiations with Canada and British Columbia. From this paper, it was evident that Dr. Mills not only recognizes deep-seated Git̲xsan concerns, but she understands them within the context of the overall history of Crown and Aboriginal relationships.

For this book, Dawn was given a series of guidelines that required the use of publicly available materials that included, but were not limited to, the evidence collected by all three parties for the trial from 1989 to 1991, the transcripts of the proceedings (the 1991 Trial, the 1993 Court of Appeal, and Commissioned Evidence), as well as any materials in the Hereditary Chiefs' Library, or forwarded to Dawn from the Hereditary Chiefs' Office. As she was writing, I received drafts on a regular basis, and commented accordingly.

For Future Generations: Reconciling Gitxsan and Canadian Law reflects, quite sincerely, Gitxsan struggles since the coming of the *Lixs giigyet* (New-comers), and especially the Gitxsan position with respect to the litigation, *Delgam'Uukw* v. *British Columbia*, and our treaty negotiation position since the Court of Appeal decision in 1993. Chronicled are the Gitxsan struggles in their attempts to forward their solution to the land question. Dawn sets out a comprehensive analysis of Gitxsan *Ayooks* of *Naa hlimoot'* which give substance to our land tenure and governance system, and how we assign access rights to resources on our *lax'wiiyip* (land) to ensure that all Gitxsan have sufficient food resources.

This book lays the groundwork for the Gitxsan to continue to forward our *ayooks* and governance principles as a treaty platform that focuses on assisting government with setting up justifiable infringement standards, joint consultation protocols, and the development of standards for the accommodation of our Aboriginal rights, which could include the determination of indices for resource-sharing revenues that would flow directly to trust accounts managed by the *Gim litxwid*. The Gitxsan further understand that there remains the option of proving their title in court and knowing their rights are bound up both in their history of occupying the territories they claim, and the management of these lands and resources according to their laws. In the event that the Gitxsan elect to take their claim of ownership back to court, this material will be extremely important.

In conclusion, I would like to say that *For Future Generations* exemplifies Dawn's ongoing commitment to reconciliation and her motivation to provide a model for collaborative land use between the Crown and Aboriginal people. I am honoured to provide this foreword for Dr. Dawn Mills, who is not only a remarkable scholar, researcher, and teacher, but also a compassionate person and friend who has shown, again and again, the importance of *Lixs giigyet* relationships and collaborations in the struggle to obtain recognition of Aboriginal rights.

Don Ryan
Hanamuxw

Introduction

My personal history is a combination of academic study and a strong family tradition of advocacy related to First Nation peoples in Canada through my mother's family, and in the United States through my father's. When it appeared that the Nisga'a were going to succeed in securing a negotiating table in the late 1980s, my uncle introduced me to the Gitxsan. I was subsequently asked by the Gitxsan to act as an observer to the litigation from 1987 to 1996, and see how they desired to conclude the land question.

For this review, I examined the arguments and the evidence, and read the proceedings of both the trial and the appeal to the British Columbia Court of Appeal. I worked often at the Gitxsan Hereditary Chiefs' Office in Vancouver, and, when possible, I attended at the courthouse to hear the proceedings firsthand. I was familiar with the successive colonial, dominion, and Canadian constitutional history of the sometimes strained relationship between First Nations in British Columbia and the political rulers of both the province and Canada, and I concluded that neither level of government was aware of the significance of the oral tradition in binding First Nations to their law, their land, and their customs — nor how they could use this knowledge in the service of both reconciliation and future relationships.

At the same time, I had to conclude that the ruling of the trial judge, contrary to the opinion of most Gitxsan at the time, yielded a monumental victory for British Columbia First Nations. It is true that Justice McEachern limited his ruling to a narrow aspect of law, yet it could be argued that the political nature of the unanswered land question motivated Victoria to re-examine its position regarding how to reconcile First Nations' unceded title with that of the Province. The Gitxsan case had gone to the Court of Appeal, but now there was a framework for negotiation. The ensuing decision laid the seeds of reconciliation in the doctrine of continuity, in as much as Gitxsan law and legal orders could be incorporated by British Columbia as a means of reconciling their past and continuing presence on their territories.

The minority decision at the Court of Appeal recognized the possibility that First Nations jurisdictions, law, and legal orders could be used for the administration of the Crowns' fiduciary obligations on First Nations lands, treaty lands, or treaty entitlement lands, creating a place for First Nations law in the Crowns' justifiable legislative imperatives. These ideas, in combination with the test that can be applied against evidence for the determination of Aboriginal title and rights developed by the Supreme Court, have quite possibly laid the foundation for reconciliation, situated not only in First Nations' rights, but also in their interests.

The 1997 *Delgam'Uukw* decision of the Supreme Court of Canada is more than ten years old, and not much has changed at the negotiating table. The "cede and surrender" model, now couched in terms of "certainty and finality," leaves to First Nations jurisdiction a truncated land base, with the expectation that this will somehow enable community members to act on their Aboriginal rights as well as engage in modern business endeavours. This model leaves little room to integrate traditional laws, procedures, and accountability, and offers little guidance on how these traditions may exist parallel with provincial administrative structures. Further, the model leaves Canada in a weakened position with respect to protecting First Nations' continued rights over those aspects of their culture, language, and laws that do not intersect with other Canadian laws and orders.

The Gitxsan have testified, in court and in public, about their governance system, their social and political institutions, and their allocation laws. They have explained their desire for Crown protection of their Aboriginal rights and title, as well as their wish to integrate their governance customs and laws with those of British Columbia and Canada in their respective jurisdictions. The Gitxsan want to enter into a formal alliance with Canada, in exchange for continued protection of their section 35 rights throughout the *lax'wiiyip* (*wilp* or house territories), reconciling their past occupation with that of the Newcomers, and forging a working relationship with the province with respect to the management of resources in, on, or below their traditional territories.

The academic literature is based overwhelmingly on the litigation, and contemporary analysis speaks only to the general reconciliation of Aboriginal rights in that context. The Gitxsan, like all citizens, look to their law as the basis for their relationship with the Crown, yet their concerns are not being heard. This book is an attempt to carry the issue forward.

Gitxsan Glossary

Adawaak: The narrative owned by a particular *wilp* or by Houses denoting both their migration back into the *wilp lax'wiiyip* and the boundaries of their particular territories.

Am bilan: Ceremonial aprons worn by the *Sigidim haanak'a* and *Simgigyet* at any one of the *yukws*, and which are passed from generation to generation.

'Am halitx: Refers to headdresses containing sea lion whiskers.

Amnigwootxw: Permission to use another's territory based on several reasons. For example, members of one's father's family can use one's mother's territory, or permission may be given for good deeds done toward the *wilp*. If children are orphaned, their *wams* are held in trust for them by another, and, in the meantime, those looking after the children are given permission to use the *wams* and *ayuks* of their *wilp* for those children's benefit.

Andemane: The name of a rocky point on the Skeena, marking a territorial boundary.

Anliidiiks: Landmarks that mark the boundary of any *wilp's lax'wiiyip*.

Andimbanak: This term refers to one's spouse's kinship group.

Anjok: The act of asking permission to use the territory of another, and is also considered to be a specific place where one dwells on the *lax'wiiyip*.

An si bilaa: The name of the fishing site that was given to the W*ilp* of *Hanamuxw* for *xsiisx* from the *Wilp* of *Luutkudziiwas'*.

Antgulilbix: Antgulilbix became the name of the young man who saved the Baby Goat. He alone was saved from the landslide that was invoked by the One-Horned Mountain Goats after the young boys taunted and tossed other Baby Mountain Goats into the fire, and this name, *Antgulilibix*, comes from the whirlpool that took the tree down.

Ax Gwin Desxw: The name of the *Xsgooim* and the *Wilp* of *Malii*.

Ayook: Laws given to the Gitxsan in order that they may co-exist with each other and the animals.

Ayuk: Symbols that represent title to particular *lax'wiiyip* or fishing sites by the *wilp*.

Biis hoon: Name of *Tenmigyet wilp's adawaak*, and the name of its central character.

Bii Lax ha: The name given by the *Wilp* of *Tenmigyet* to Charlie Smith, giving him *amnigwootxw* rights on *Tenmigyet's lax'wiiyip*, while his *wilp* cared for the *Tenmigyet's wilp's* orphaned children. It is also the name of another village that *Biis hoon* had to start, as her bear children were hard to live around.

Daawxiis: Contribution made to a *wilp* for the immediate use of a fishing site, berry patch, or hunting territory.

Dam ana koots: An area of *Txa'axwok's lax'wiiyip* especially good for trapping beaver.

Dawamuxw: The name of the *Xsgooim* and the *Wilp* of *Dawamuxw*.

Dax gyet: Power and authority of the *Sigidim haanak'a* and *Simgigyet* to delegate in the name of the *wilp,* and also in the name of all Gitxsan people.

Dax yuk dit lax yip: Refers to the caretaker of the territory until a debt is cleared.

Deex iiyasxw: Strings that are attached to the baskets of the women who are berry picking on another's *lax'wiiyip*; they indicate that permission has been given to them by the *wilp's Sigidim haanak'a* and *Simgigyet*.

Delgam'Uukw: Person's *wilp* name.

Ee dim uma yees: On the breath of your ancestor.

Gaak: Raven.

Gawa gyanii: This is the peace or treaty process that is made between the Gitxsan and their neighbours, as well a amongst themselves to settle a inter-*wilp* feud or war.

Geddun-cal-doe: The name of one of the *Simgigyets* who petitioned on behalf of *Haatq* for the killing of Youmans.

Galaa'uu: He is the brother who killed *'Wiihloots*.

Gal dim algyak: Speaker at a *yukw*.

Gelenk: Special storage boxes that hold *Sigidim haanak'a* and *Simgigyet* ceremonial regalia that were opened to the *Lixs giigyet* during the *Delgam'Uukw* proceedings, 1987 to 1990.

Genada: The Frog Clan.

Gim litxwid: The alliance of Gitxsan *Sigidim haanak'a* and *Simgigyet,* as well as referring to the Gitxsan National Government.

Gisday Wa: The *kungax* of the house of *Gisday Wa* talks about the people coming from the east when a bow and arrow fight takes place between the Wet'suwet'en and the Naskoteen peoples.

Gisk'aast: The Fireweed Clan.

Git lax an dek': An ancient village where the *wilp* of *Tenmigyet* originates.

Gitludahl: One of the four *huwilp* that come from the *pteex* of *Gisk'aast*.

Gitsegukla: *A Gitxsan Village,* and now a Reserve community.

Gus maga 'mix kaax: The returning of the down, or the feather.

Gwaans: A name that means, "When the eagle flies around and lands on top of the tree." This is a chiefly name in the W*ilp* of *Hanamuxw*.

Gwiis gan 'malaa: Blanket robes.

Gwiiyeehl: The name of the *Xsgooim* and the *Wilp* of *Gwiiyeehl*.

Gwis Gyen: The name of the *Wilp* of *Gwis Gyen* and means "little pitch." This wilp adopted the stranger, who lived with his sister and named him *Waigyet*.

Gwin o'op: A fishing site that belongs to the *Wilp* of *Hawow* at the confluence of the Kispiox and Skeena River.

Gyanimx: Refers to contemporary Gitxsan language.

Gyologyet: A chiefly name of the *Xsgooim Sigidim haanak'a* and *Simgigyet* of the *Wilp* of *Gyologyet*, meaning, "to stand in one accord."

Haalus: *Ax Gwin Desxw's* father-in-law, and the name of the *Xsgooim* and the *Wilp* of *Haalus*.

Haat'ixslaxnox: One of the adawaaks owned by the *Wilp* of *Haatq*.

Haatq: The name of the Gitxsan man who killed Youmans for the wrongful death of his son, Billy Owens.

Ha'atxw: The name of the person who killed *'Niitsxw*.

Halayt: The power in the crest and ceremony.

Hanamuxw: One of the houses of *Gisk'aast* established in *Gitsegukla*; they hold the *Adawaak* of *Ska 'wo* (the man in a hat, who is covered with stars).

Hauxw: Spring salmon.

Hidinsim Getingan: The series of feasts for raising a pole.

Hlho'oxs: The name of a creek on the *lax'wiiyip* of the *Wilp* of *Gyologyet*.

Hlaa niin xsi gyalatxwit dim ant guuhl hli dax gyets dip niye'en. Dim guudinhl wa midim'y ama gya'adihl Lax yip: The recipient is the one who has been selected to take the inheritable land, to hold it, and to take care of it.

Huwilp: Plural of *wilp*.

K'aat': Staff used to indicate that permission has been given to the person to be on the *lax'wiiyip* of another.

Kamalmuk: The name of the man who killed *Neatsqu*.

K'i'yhl luuks: Refers to bundles of 40.

Kungax: Dances of the Wet'suwet'en that holds the history of the House group.

Kwamoo: The name of a creek on the *lax'wiiyip* of the *Wilp* of *Gyologyet*.

Laan: The name of a person from the *Wilp* of *Dawamuxw*.

Laxgibuu: The Wolf Clan.

Laxsel: The Raven Clan.

Laxskiik: The Eagle clan.

Lax'wiiyip: The traditional territories of the Gitxsan and Gitxsen people, located around the upper Skeena and Nass watershed, and encompassing the Bulkley, Babine, and Kispiox Rivers.

Legaix: Tsimshian chief who created a trading network among the Nisga'a and Gitxsan through marriage.

Lelt: The name of the *Xsgooim* and the *Wilp* of *Lelt*.

Ligigalwil: One of the two persons who were killed by the Stikine.

Ligii will: Food presents given to the guest at the end of a *yukw*.

Li'ligit: The feast complex of the Gitxsan.

Limxoo'y: Songs that all *wilps* posses that are sung at the death of a *Xsgooim*. These songs "send one off on the breath of our forefathers."

Lixs giigyet: Those who came from away; newcomers; those who are not Gitxsan.

Luu skadakwit: An area of *Txaaxwok's lax'wiiyip* which is especially good for hunting moose, bear, and ground squirrels.

Luu ska'yan't: A specific place on *Waiget's lax'wiiyip*.

Luutkudziiwas': After the killing of a member of the *Wilp* of *Hanamuxw*, *Luutkudziiwas'* gave them the fishing station, *An si bilaa*.

Ma'uus: The name of the *Xsgooim* and the *Wilp* of *Ma'uus*.

Maa'yaast: The name of the colourful trimming given to women to put on their baskets, indicating that permission has been given to use the berry grounds.

Madiigim gyetu: A member of the *Wilp* of *Spookw'*.

Malii: The name of this *wilp* refers to the *adawaak* of the two bear cubs/children *Biis hoon* brought back after her brother killed their father. The cubs and *Biis hoon* were banished from their village, as the bears could not easily live around humans.

Mediik: A mythical grizzly bear that lives in the lake at the foot of *Stekyooden*.

Mix k'aax: Part of the settlement process instigated after issues between families or nations have escalated to killing, and this speaks of the spreading of Eagle Down.

Naa hlimoot': Laws of sharing that set out how food is divided among the community and the practice of helping one another.

Nax nox: The power within a person, which is expressed throughout life; it is contained in the *wams*, the *ayuks*, and the *adawaaks*, and acted out at the *yukws*.

Neatsqu: The name of the shaman who was killed by *Kamalmuk* (also known as Kitwancool Jim) for bringing a curse onto his family.

'Nii dil: The person who stands up for you and advises you when you receive an important *wam*.

Niis Noohl: Name of the person who was given *amnigwootxw* rights on *Tenmigyet's lax'wiiyip*, as he was the son of the departed *Simgigyet*.

'Niitsxw: The name of the person from the *Wilp* of *Hanamuxw* who was killed by *Ha'atxw*.

Pteex: This term refers to one of the four, or related, clans in Gitxsan society.

Saagit: When one habitually trespasses onto another *wilp's lax'wiiyip*, one may be beaten to death and the family cannot retaliate, and *saagit* is the official version of a murder.

Sakxum Higookx: Both the name of a *wilp* and the name of a person bestowed by their *wilp*.

Sduutwx'm Lax ha: The name of the *Xsgooim* and the *Wilp* of *Sduutwx'm Lax ha*.

She-quin-khatt: The name of a creek that flows into the Skeena, marking a territorial boundary.

Sigidim haanak'a: A female person who holds the name of the *wilp*.

Simgigyet: A male person who holds the name of the *wilp*.

Sim algyax: An ancient Gitxsan language.

Sinankxws: The name *Sinankxws* was held by Fanny Williams at the time of the Trial and is the process of seeking the advice of other Gitxsan *Xsgooim*.

Sisixsek: "Pulling the chiefs out" to resolve a dispute that encompasses all the communities.

Siyehl widit: A curse that will be brought onto one's *wilp* for fighting over food.

Skoogm hon: The first spring salmon caught in a village, which is carefully laid on a mat, carried to the village, cooked, and distributed to all, while giving thanks to the salmon for returning.

Spookw': A Gitxsan *wilp*.

Stekyooden: A mountain in Gitxsan territory where the historic city of *T'am Lax amit* was located, and this means, "one stands alone."

T'aam Gins xhoux: A body of water now known as Sand Lake.

Tamis maa'yaast: The name of a lake in *Tenmigyet's lax'wiiyip* that has a blue clay bed.

T'am Lax amit: The name of the city that the Gitxsan had lived in before the disasters occurred.

Tenmigyet: The name of the youngest brother who rescued *Biis hoon* and became *Wii Sigidim haanak'a* and *Simgigyet*; the name means "half human and half bear."

T'ewelasxw: The name of a person who lent *Tenmigyet* a boat to catch spring salmon.

T'saan: The general name for memorial poles.

Tsibasaa: The brother of *Antgulilbix*.

Tsihl Gwellii: A place on *Tenmigyet's Lax'wiiyip* where *'mili kooxst* grows (berries).

Ts'ii yee: The name of the person from the *Wilp* of *Gwis gyen* who helped the *Wilp* of *Tenmigyet* with funeral expenses.

Tsimxsan: Now known as the Tsimshian language.

Tss'uu wijix: When the laws of sharing were broken when the brothers of *Tenmigyet* fought over the kill of the caribou and brought a curse on their *wilp*.

Txawok: One of the two persons killed by the Stikine.

Txaaxwok: The name of the *Xsgooim* and the *Wilp* of *Txaaxwok*.

Wa'ayin wam: A name given to a person in order that they may enter a *yukw*.

Waiget: The name of the *Xsgooim* and the *Wilp* of *Waiget*.

Wam: A name given to a person at birth. Throughout their lives they may be given other names, reflecting altered status. All "*wams*" given are owned by the *wilp*.

Wii Eelast: The name of the *Xsgooim* and the *Wilp* of *Wii Eelast*.

'Wiihloots: He was killed by his brother, *Gallaa'uu*.

Wii Sigidim haanak'a and *Simgigyet*: Another term for the name of the chief who holds the house name.

Wilksiwitxw: One's father's family. It is one's father's family that provides one's first and last bed, one's cradle and coffin. One's father's family is also responsible for one's early education, as well as providing money to one's mother's family at *yukws* throughout one's lifetime and sponsoring the feast where one receives names.

Wil'na t'ahl: The extended matrilineal family, though this may be in a different *wilp*, they hold the same *pteex* membership.

Wilp: The primary property holding unit in Gitxsan society. The term *wilp* has been used in the past to describe the natal family as well as a living dwelling. More importantly, a *wilp* are all family members that a person — including all aunts, uncles and cousins — can trace through his or her maternal grandmother.

Win skahl Guuhl: A specific territory on *Gyologyet's lax'wiiyip*.

Xai mooksisim: The name of the feast held at the first snowfall by the *Laxgibuu pteex* of each village.

Xamlaxyeltxw: This name means, "when people go wading into the water."

Xhliimlaxha: The name of the *Xsgooim* of the *Wilp* of *Xhliimlaxha,* and means "walks across the sky."

Xkyeehl: Rights to resources in exchange for gifts — money, prestige objects — given in front of the community at a *yukw* to show appreciation.

Xsagangaxda: The place where *Yal* was killed, where the creek flows into the river on the ice.

Xsi gwin ixst'aat: The name of the village where *Tenmigyet* lived.

Xsiisx: Compensation given for an intentional or accidental death which could range anywhere from land exchange to being given a name.

Xsi maxhla saa Giibax: The name of the territory turned over to *Waiget* by the *Wilp* of *Sduutxw'lax* to pay for funerals.

Xsinaahlxw: A breath song of a *Xsgooim*

Xsgooim: Another term associated with the head *Sigidim haanak'a* and *Simgigyet*.

Yal: The name of the *Xsgooim* and the *Wilp* of *Yal*.

Yukw: General term associated with a feast.

Yuugwilatxw: Extending rights to one's spouse.

CHAPTER ONE

Be Gentle on the Newcomers

AUTHOR'S NOTE: In a conversation with *Wii Eelast* in January 1998, I was asked to be gentle on the *Lixs giigyet* (Newcomers), "for they are like children in the territories." The Gitxsan had for years been rescuing them from the bush when they were lost or in trouble, and had concluded that it was important to know who was on the *lax'wiiyip* in order that they may be safe. This policy of treating the Newcomers with respect and assisting them in troubled times is in keeping with the generosity of the Gitxsan, and is reflected in the attitude of Indigenous peoples across the continent toward Newcomers arriving in their territory.

ON 22 OCTOBER 1984, THE GITXSAN AND WET'SUWET'EN FILED A STATEMENT OF claim against the province of British Columbia, seeking a declaration that they had the right of ownership of, and jurisdiction over, their house territories (*wilp lax'wiiyip*). The statement of claim was filed at the Smithers Registry in the name of *Delgam'Uukw*, which was held at that time by Albert Tait. They felt they had exhausted all other means of negotiating an agreement with the federal and provincial governments to settle the question of their house territories. The plaintiffs — 35 Gitxsan and 13 Wet'suwet'en hereditary chiefs (*Simgigyet* and *Sigidim haanak'a*[1]) — alleged that, since time immemorial, they had occupied and held jurisdiction over approximately 58,000 square kilometres in northwest British Columbia. They sought a judgement that they had ownership of and jurisdiction over 133 separate territories: 98 Gitxsan and 35 Wet'suwet'en.

The chief underlying issue was that the Crown had not lived up to its obligation of ensuring that the property laws of First Nations were integrated into the federal-provincial constitutional framework; thus, First Nations communities were left outside the decision-making process regarding the disposition of land and resources in their traditional territories. Aboriginal people have made many attempts to bring this lack of acknowledgement of their property laws and institutions of self-government to the attention of Canada. The Crown's agents have looked at specific grievances and situations, and have at times attempted redress. Such negotiated solutions, however, have not included equitable long-term settlements, including revenue-sharing based on the use of First Nations' lands for the settlement of newcomers.

For the Gitxsan, reconciliation lies in sharing jurisdictional authority among Canada and British Columbia in order that they may use the resource and property allocation principles embedded in their *Ayooks* of *Naa hlimoot'* (laws of sharing). Specifically, Canada could achieve jurisdictional certainty by having the Gitxsan grant *amnigwootxw* rights, or privileged access, throughout their territories. British Columbia and the Gitxsan could similarly establish a viable relationship by settling consultation protocols, infringement guidelines, and indices for compensation situated in Gitxsan principles of *xkyeehl*,[2] or payments, throughout the Gitxsan statement-of-claim area. The Gitxsan could then give assurance to Canada that their traditional governance structure, the *wilp* system, is situated in democratic principles. The communities' decision-making process through the *Gim litxwid* alliance of *huwilp* (all houses) allows the Gitxsan people the opportunity to counsel their leaders through polling opinions.

It has been suggested that the current perspective on the status of Aboriginal title, as laid out by the Supreme Court, is sufficiently broad to negotiate an agreement based on Gitxsan *lax'wiiyip* ownership and governance principles, which are outlined in the *Acts of Reconciliation*.[3] Drawing on the underlying principle of reconciliation as articulated by Chief Justice Lamer in *R. v. Van der Peet*,[4] British Columbia, Canada, and the Gitxsan people can build administrative relationships and develop the resources in the territories for the benefit of the Gitxsan and the newcomers alike. From this flows the conclusion that the principal Aboriginal right of the Gitxsan is to be able to act within their legal and governance structures when engaging with either the provincial or federal governments in the allocation and administration of resources throughout the *lax'wiiyip*.

When the Gitxsan went to Court in 1987, it was generally accepted in Canada that Aboriginal title referred to the interest, unsurrendered by treaty or unextinguished by legislation, of Aboriginal peoples to lands they traditionally used and occupied.⁵ Aboriginal title is considered *sui generis* in nature, as it does not originate in English, French, or First Nation property law. It appears that what determines the quality of Aboriginal title, then, is the nature of the surrender, not the content of the title before declarations of sovereignty by the Crown. This suggests that only First Nations communities who have sought the "protection of the Crown,"⁶ agreed "to be subjects of the Crown,"⁷ or contracted to "follow the regulations stipulated by the Crown from time to time"⁸ need modify their definition of territory, title, or governance.⁹ Besides Aboriginal title lands associated with treaties, surrenders and reserves, Aboriginal title is also considered site specific where Aboriginal rights activities, such as hunting, fishing, and trapping outside the reserve, occur subject to Crown regulation. The Crown presently recognizes the rights of First Nations to hunt, fish, trap, and gather food in areas of their traditional use and occupancy. Although the courts have accepted that Aboriginal title constitutes a proprietary interest in the land, they have also held that these rights may, in some situations, be modified or abridged by federal and provincial fisheries and wildlife legislation. Recently, the courts have accepted in theory that Aboriginal title, like Aboriginal rights, exists until surrendered or is modified by treaty, legislation, or land claim agreements. The rights to land and its use of communities who have yet to enter into agreements are still subject to a case-by-case evaluation.

Before 1997, it was generally assumed that the presence of the Crown had replaced First Nations' land interests on Crown lands through the categorical denial of title to First Nations and the annexation of what were considered "waste lands." The Gitxsan, though they do not farm, as such, have clear boundaries that delineate the internal divisions of their *wilp* territories, as well as clearly marked territorial boundaries with their neighbours. These boundaries, both internal and external, are marked in a variety of ways, from stone columns to blazed trees, and from running creeks to specific, named locations. The Gitxsan also cultivated berry patches, used specific fishing sites, hunted animals in particular passes, knew the locations of bear dens, and practised selective harvesting of beaver and ground squirrels. The Gitxsan, individually and as a group, know the sum total of their land through occupation and use. Title, tenure, and legitimate use of Gitxsan land and resources are determined by birth, affinity, common residence, social status, or a combination of these. Those who cannot demonstrate knowledge of its history through the recitation of the *adawaak* (oral histories) and knowledge of the *ayuk(s)* (symbols of title) cannot claim rights to it. The Gitxsan have a system to determine who is a member of a particular *wilp,* and a process that determines the allocation of *wilp* resources. They also have a body of law that regulates access, use, and the distribution of resources from any one *wilp lax'wiiyip* to the broader community.

As Gitxsan law regulates how *wilp* members are to use *wilp lax'wiiyip,* they also have regulations that govern how secondary and tertiary rights are granted to individuals outside the *wilp.* Further, mechanisms within their law permit them to alienate or encumber their territory. Although these laws are limited, they do not diminish or abrogate the original owners' right to the territory in question as their own, or in some cases restore the territory to the *wilp.* Finally, the Gitxsan have the means to ensure that individuals use the land and resources in accordance with the availability of the resource in question, and in a manner that does not endanger the security of the group, insofar as the consequence of a particular action can be foreseen.

Like other Aboriginal communities across North America, the Gitxsan have occupied distinct territories according to systematic hunting, fishing, trapping, and gathering patterns over long periods, and they also have stable systems of political authority, land tenure, and resource harvesting. Other Canadian Aboriginal people, such as the Mi'kmaq, Denneza, and Inuit, have claims to tenure that are closely related to the subsistence resource, as well as their political and social organization. There is a common theme among these societies: individuals are required to self-regulate their activities, and any person who steps too far from the normal expected behaviours runs the risk of being ostracized. Every person knows and observes the laws about how, where, and when to hunt, fish, or trap, as well as how to listen to the counsel of others regarding hunting matters. When conflicts need to be resolved, the emphasis is on mediation and compromise.

It might appear that the individual's rights in Aboriginal societies lie in the products, not in the territory itself, but this does not take into account the sense of belonging to particular locations, or the relationship between the human and the animal. For the Mi'kmaq, Denneza, and Inuit, these feelings of belonging to a location are born out of the distinct history they share with the territory in question, where the territory itself is infused with anthropomorphic characteristics as well as layered with personal events involving their ancestors. When people appeared in the regions, they found the animals already there, and considered themselves to be moving into an existing society; thus, the relationship between human and animal is interwoven, as humankind derives its status, according to Richard Preston, not by seeking dominance over animals, but according to the competence and particular needs of the "other persons" — and these "persons" are animals, fish, plant life, and the land itself.[10] Frank Speck has suggested that the Mi'kmaq view animal life as tribal and similar to that of humans, only animals do not have humankind's "technical gifts and powers."[11] For the Denneza, according to Scott Rushford, the land has been transformed by their ancestors into a place that is able to support their life.[12] The Denneza believe that the animals themselves taught them how they are to be captured for food, and how to secure their continued presence.[13] Similarly, as Knud Rasmussen has explained, the Inuit are born of the animals and spirits, who know their need to be brought into the human sphere, both through capture and the respect that the animals must be shown at the time of their death.[14]

Although the Supreme Court of Canada in *Delgam'Uukw*[15] enlarged the quality of Aboriginal title to encompass forestry and mining, at the same time the Gitxsan and other First Nations have not been able to obtain the legal redress necessary to sustain their traditional use rights — hunting, fishing, trapping, and gathering food for social or ceremonial use — following the destruction or degradation of the habitat by third parties who have obtained competing rights from the Crown. The Gitxsan, despite their dependency on fish and wildlife, have acquired no special power to allocate, regulate, or manage these resources under provincial or federal management programs that will ensure their continued access.

Administrative policy and practice has for years been based on the assumption that Aboriginal rights and title have effectively conferred no more than a license to enter into an area, and even this right is not held to be exclusive. Current federal and provincial treaty-making processes still expect the First Nation community to further identify lands to be set aside for their exclusive use and to surrender their rights and title to their traditional territories in exchange for access to specific Aboriginal right activity sites, subject to Crown jurisdiction. In *Haida* v. *British Columbia*[16] and *Mikisew Cree* v. *British Columbia*,[17] for example, the Supreme Court has taken the perspective that, although the government may not "run rough-shod" over Aboriginal rights, treaty, or title where the community may have a *prima facie* claim, neither the Gitxsan nor any other First Nation has the right to veto the proposed development pending final proof of their claim. These rulings, like *Delgam'Uukw*, expect a negotiated resolution in which the Crown is "bound to balance societal and Aboriginal interests in making decisions that may affect Aboriginal claims," and "may be required to make decisions in the face of disagreement as to the adequacy of its response to Aboriginal concerns."[18]

Focusing on the history of the Gitxsan and newcomer relationship, Gitxsan political authority has been compromised since the assertion of sovereignty by the newcomers in 1846, and the Crown has displaced the *Sigidim haanak'a* and *Simgigyet* as the owners and managers of the *huwilp lax'wiiyip*. In general, First Nations communities have had few opportunities in either the historic treaties or contemporary land claims agreements to integrate their laws and administration into either provincial or federal law. The Gitxsan have testified as to their governance system, their social and political institutions, their allocation laws, and their desire for Crown protection of their Aboriginal rights and titles throughout their traditional territories. More importantly, their testimony has highlighted their desire to integrate their governance and laws with those of British Columbia in the area of resource management, and those of Canada with respect to fish, migratory birds, and environmental protection.

The Gitxsan desire to enter into a formal alliance with Canada in exchange for continued protection of their section 35 rights throughout their *lax'wiiyip*, in order to reconcile their past occupation with that of the newcomers, and to enter into a working relationship with the Province of British Columbia with respect to the management of the resources in their traditional territories.

CHAPTER TWO

Since the Coming of the *Lixs giigyet*

THE GITXSAN HAVE LIVED IN THE SKEENA, BULKLEY, AND KISPIOX WATERSHEDS since time immemorial. When everyone lived at *T'am Lax amit*, a great village along the Skeena River that extended from present-day Gitsegukla to Kispiox, the animals, fish, plants, and humans were able to communicate, and each had a clear understanding of how they submitted to each other. As time wore on, however, the humans over-hunted. According to the Gitxsan *adawaaks* (oral histories),[1] the mountain goats invited the people to a feast. Even at the feast, the humans continued to disrespect the goats, and killed them without shame. The goats brought the mountain of *Stekyooden* down around the Gitxsan in retaliation. Later, at the lake at the foot of *Stekyooden* after salmon fishing season was over, the young ladies played with the bones of some of the trout they had caught. This disrespect for the remains of the trout aroused the wrath of *Mediik,* and in his rage he caused a great flood, clearing the land of people.[2] The people left at *T'am Lax amit* continued to ignore the warnings of the Sun God, one of the Gitxsan deities. It was the time when the spring salmon return to their *huwilp*, and the Gitxsan allowed a young boy to poke fun at the sky. Even though it was late spring, it started to snow. The sky did not like the taunts, and at the request of the Sun God, brought more snows, creating the glaciers.[3]

It was at this time that the larger animals — bear, mountain goat, wolf, deer, and mountain lion — wanted to rid the world of the humans and prevent them from returning. However, the smaller animals — skunk, ground squirrel, raccoon, and mouse — felt this was a bit harsh and lobbied for a negotiated agreement, as they were rarely taken by the humans and relied on them for their existence. The compromise the animals worked out was that the people of *T'am Lax amit* were to be banished from the territories until they had learned not to over-hunt, not to disrespect the animals or desecrate the lands, and were able to follow the *ayooks* (laws).[4] Winter lasted a long time. When the people emerged from under the ice and snow their land was changed; it was like new. It was at this time that pine trees moved into the region. Each group followed those they could understand,[5] so some went in different directions. Each group was told to follow the laws. They were told not to over-hunt, to be respectful of remains, to respect each other, and, above all, to respect the memory of their banishment.

Regional indigenous politics and property laws for the most part have set the stage for the peaceful integration of *Lixs giigyet* (those who came from away, newcomers) on the coast and in the interior of the Pacific Northwest after 1787. Early inter-cultural relations were centred mainly on the business of provisioning ships, the maritime fur trade, and interior trade as it was established by the North West Company after 1795 and along the Pacific coast by the Hudson's Bay Company after 1821. These early relations were controlled through the social and political structures of the Tsimshian, Nisga'a, Gitxsan, and Sekani. In each of these societies it was always publicly known where each house and family territory was, and the nature of the resources on it. In addition, it was understood that each *wilp's* title was entrenched in a legal system that regulated rights of access to members of the *wilp* in each village as well as relatives who lived beyond their territory. It was incumbent on the *Simgigyet* and *Sigidim haanak'a* of the leading *wilp* within each village, along with his or her advisors and the headman of the other *huwilp*, to manage the overall economy and labour requirements of the village, as well as relations with other villages.

The Arrival of the *Lixs giigyet*: Regional Economy: 1795–1910

The *Lixs giigyet* traded metal tools, copper sheeting, guns, cloth, and other luxury items for sea otter pelts on the coast from the 1780s until about 1800.[6] By 1805, the North West Company had established inland fur trading posts at Fort MacLeod, and, by 1807, had established Fort George and Fort St. James.[7] European goods were filtering into Gitxsan territory from the coast through Tsimshian and Nisga'a trade and by established trading networks with the Sekani to the east.

By 1822, in an effort to trade directly with the Gitxsan, the Hudson's Bay Company, having merged with the North West Company in 1821, established Fort Kilmaurs at the head of Babine Lake. It was not until 1826, however, that

Hudson's Bay trader William Brown visited three Gitxsan villages. Brown reported that the Gitxsan *Simgigyet* were "much attached" to the Coastal Indian traders, and also observed that they were better dressed and their fishing techniques more sophisticated than those of the Carrier communities, now known as the Wet'suwet'en, east of the Gitxsan. Brown also commented that the Gitxsan, like the Carriers, cremated their dead and put feasts on for "the deposit of the bones." More importantly, the Gitxsan were "men of property," in that they held specific tracts of land that were reserved exclusively for personal *wilp* use. Brown also observed that access, hunting, or trapping was strictly regulated by the *Simgigyet* and *Sigidim haanak'a*,[8] and contingent on the salmon returns; that is, in years when the salmon were plentiful, the Gitxsan did not hunt early in the fall, but postponed their trapping until mid-winter instead of immediately dispersing throughout their territories after the "pinks" had returned.[9]

More often than not, when the Bay traders reached the Forks — the confluence of the Skeena and Bulkley Rivers — they were told that other traders from the coast had already been to the villages, and there were not many quality furs left. During this early period, 1821-1840, when the Hudson's Bay Company was desirous of acquiring more trade in the region, it tried to position forts in the area surrounding Gitxsan villages. Despite this, the Company traders quickly found that they were unable to make direct contact with the Gitxsan, as other First Nations guides would not trespass. Historians Robert Galois and Susan Marsden assert that part of the Company's failure to gain control of the trade in the region was owing to the fact that they were unable to reorient the Gitxsan exchange networks — that is to say, the Tsimshian *Simgigyet Legaix* and his family held the trading monopoly, through marriage as well as by force within the Nisga'a and Gitxsan communities.[10]

According to A. J. Ray, it appeared that, until Brown found high quality moose hides, which were greatly prized by the Gitxsan, the Hudson's Bay Company could not compete with the traditional practices or trading allies of the Gitxsan. The Company obtained moose hides from trading districts east of the Rocky Mountains, particularly in the Athabasca-Mackenzie area. The Gitxsan valued these hides for use in their funeral feasts. According to Brown, they chopped up the leather and distributed it at the time of the burning of the body. Only the highest quality was acceptable, and if the leather was given away when "the bones were disposed," the skins were distributed whole. Large white skins were preferred, for which the Gitxsan would pay almost any price.[11] However, the Company could not induce the Gitxsan, the Wet'suwet'en, or the Sekani to trap more beaver than was permitted by their *Simgigyet*. Thus, regardless of the quality or quantity of these hides, the trade in beaver remained sporadic, and contingent on salmon surpluses, as regulated by the *Simgigyets*.

During this time, the *Lixs giigyet* had a minor presence in the interior, and only a few stayed for any length of time, even after the British purportedly consolidated their interests in the northwest as a result of the Oregon Boundary Treaty in 1846[12] and the merging of the Mainland and the Vancouver Island colony in 1862. The Gitxsan were interested in trading with the *Lixs giigyet* and sharing other business possibilities, and brought to the attention of Mr. McNeill, Fort Simpson's commander, the presence of gold up the Skeena. As McNeill noted in his journal on April 8, 1852,

> this day one of the Chiefs from Skeena River that arrived here yesterday, brought a few SMALL pieces of Gold ore to the fort, two large pieces of Quartz Rock with a few particles of Gold ore. . . . He tells that the gold is to be seen in many places on the surface of the Rock for some distance, say two miles. This is a most important discovery, at least I think so.[13]

Several years later, during the tenure of Governor James Douglas, this discovery prompted the commission of Mr. W. Downie to explore the Skeena River, taking note of potential mineral prospects. Downie found gold and coal seams, and met Gitxsan from the villages of Gitsegukla (Kitsegukla), Gitanmaax (Kittamarks), Kispiox (Kispyattes), Glen Vowell (Anlagasimdex), Naas Glee, and Kithathatts.

"We experienced some dangers from Indians here," Downie wrote in 1859, "but by a small present of tobacco, and by a determined and unconcerned aspect, I succeeded in avoiding the danger of collision with them."[14]

Galois suggests that, when Downie gave presents, he understood that he was respecting Gitxsan law and paying for safe passage through Gitxsan territories.[15] Likewise, when the Collins Overland Telegraph was constructed in the Kispiox–Hagwilget area (1863-1867), the company negotiated safe passage by paying tolls, accommodating the expense as part of doing business. During the construction of the telegraph line, Gitxsan men enjoyed steady employment as labourers and packers.[16]

As the Collins Overland Telegraph route was shelved in favour of the Trans-Atlantic Cable in 1867, the area did not flourish as anticipated. However, a small Hudson's Bay Company trading house opened at Hagwilget in 1866. It closed in 1868, but the trader, Thomas Hankin, stayed on, and after 1871 was commissioned by the new provincial government to improve the trails in the area, again employing Gitxsan men. The economy of the region picked up again after gold was discovered in the Omineca area, northeast of Gitxsan territory, in 1871.[17]

These early relations were joint business ventures, in which each party was motivated by profit, and it could be argued that the regional economy was enhanced by the presence of the *Lixs giigyet*, though they were few in number and limited to fort areas. While the *Lixs giigyet* organized the fur trade, the improvement of trails, road construction, and eventually rail lines, the First Nations communities produced the furs and made up the bulk of the contracted labour. Employment ranged from packing, guiding, and trail construction to maintenance, which the Gitxsan regulated within their communities, making sure that *huwilp* trespass laws were strictly enforced.[18] It could be said that the introduction of employment and cash payments for seasonal work and fur only augmented the effective use of traditional resources, which were, in turn, regulated by the *Simgigyets*. Besides the introduction of European and Asian goods, and other trade and employment opportunities, Gitxsan use of alternative employment gave them a reputation for being industrious and advanced by the standards of the time

In the early contact period, *ca.* 1747-1862, Gitxsan economic and political life was relatively unaffected by the presence of the *Lixs giigyet*, although it must be pointed out that the Gitxsan, like other First Nations, were vulnerable to European diseases such smallpox, measles, and influenza, which took enormous tolls on their communities. Even so, it is generally accepted that the presence of the newcomers enhanced the livelihood of all community members. After 1862, however, tensions with respect to trespass, competing jurisdictions, and the application of British-Canadian justice emerged. The Crown, whether colonial, provincial, or dominion, did not understand Gitxsan law with respect to normative concepts of justice, nor the community's right to manage resources according to their laws in their territory.

Tensions Between the *Lixs giigyet* and the Gitxsan: 1871–1884

While the Gitxsan were embedded in the regional economy at and before the time of Confederation, tensions began to emerge soon afterward. Between 1871 and 1884, when they were feeling the effects of the region being opened up to newcomers for alternative uses, such as mining and transportation, there were clashes with respect to whose property and whose laws were valid. The Gitxsan, believing themselves sovereign, felt the *Lixs giigyet* were ignoring their laws and looking to their own. Unaware of Gitxsan laws concerning property, trespass, and justice, the *Lixs giigyet* moved freely throughout the region, unhampered by the protocols expected of them from the Gitxsan.

The Gitxsan, like other west coast societies, had specific laws and procedures governing access to and use of any piece of territory. In general, permission had to be sought to travel on, or take resources from, another's territory. If one failed to observe these protocols, one ran the risk of being beaten to death. There were also laws governing the conduct of persons in the presence of the death of others. In the case of accidental death in the company or employ of a non-family member, it is the responsibility of those present to justify the death to the *wilp* chief. If this is not done within a specified time, one runs the risk of being killed by the mourning family. In addition, if one person curses another, and the threatened one succumbs before payment is made to undo the curse, the wronged family has the right to retaliate. These laws were outside the practice of Anglo-Canadian law and justice, whose officials made little attempt to discover the intentions of Gitxsan property law and codes related to justifiable homicide.

A Conflict of Laws

By 1872, a few *Lixs giigyet* had come into the region and established businesses in Hazelton. Relations were generally good. However, a fire at Gitsegukla (Kitsegukla) and a series of justifiable homicides created tensions. The situations in themselves were minor, but they brought to the surface the tensions caused by the continued presence of the newcomers without formal relationships having been established.

The fire at Gitsegukla, in June 1872, caused an estimated loss of several thousand dollars. The Gitxsan petitioned the government:

> Two canoes passing up the river with white men in them stopped and built a fire immediately above our village. The weather being very dry for some time would have caused a fire to spread very quickly unless care was taken when leaving camp to see that it was safe. This fire was neglected by those camped there and the consequence was, the total destruction of the village, 11 houses and 13 poles, also ten canoes. The

poles are of great value to us. Our loss is very heavy, and thousands of dollars worth of property and years of time having been expended in the building of the houses and the erection of the poles, all of which was entirely destroyed in one hour by the fire.[19]

The Gitxsan blockaded the Skeena, vowing that no white man should pass, and pressing demands for restitution. By July 1, 1872, Thomas Hankin of Hazelton had compiled an inventory of what had been lost in the fire, and set out certain promises that the government ought to fulfill. The river was re-opened to freight and passenger traffic pending the arrival of a magistrate to settle the matter.[20] Later that summer, Lieutenant-Governor Joseph Trutch travelled up the coast in the gunboat *H.M.S. Scout* as far as Skeenamouth-Metlakatla for a meeting with the Gitxsan. In an elaborate show of arms and ceremony, and with William Duncan as interpreter, the province gave $600 to the *Simgigyets* — as an "act of grace," not of compensation — and warned the *Simgigyets* to speak within the law, by which was meant the Queen's law.[21]

For the Gitxsan, the issue had been concluded satisfactorily. The *Simgigyets* interpreted the public presentation of the gift of money, the show of arms, and the ceremony as the *Lixs giigyet* accepting responsibility for the fire. The events aboard *H.M.S. Scout* were compatible with Gitxsan procedures for resolving conflicts: first, there was a meeting between both sides in which they voiced their concerns; second, a settlement was reached and compensation was made; and third, both sides displayed their power by an entertainment that had elements of hospitality and spectacle. For the government, the lieutenant-governor was able to extract an agreement that the Gitsegukla *Simgigyets* would not threaten the *Lixs giigyet* by blockading the river.

Gitxsan concerns continued to grow around issues of trespass and employment. William Humphrey, in charge of the construction of a cattle trail north of Kispiox, reported in June 1874 that the Kuldoe Indians would not allow his Indian packers any further up the trail toward the settlement, nor would the Kuldoe pack without doubling the fees.[22] Reports later that year stated that Kispiox Gitxsan regularly molested the *Lixs giigyet* as they used Gitxsan trails without permission and consumed resources without compensation. Although there were several meetings with *Simgigyets*, little was resolved. One community member was eventually arrested for assault and, after appearing before William Duncan at Port Essington, was imprisoned for a month.[23] The harassment of travellers continued, however, and in 1875 Rev. Robert

Tomlinson was asked to look into the reasons for the escalating tensions in the Hazelton area. Tomlinson observed that, since the slowdown in the Peace River Mines, most Gitxsan men were out of pack work. During the gold excitement, Gitxsan men had been making hundreds of dollars as packers and guides, but by 1875, they were hardly making a tenth of that. This sudden drop in income, according to Tomlinson's journal, resulted in Gitxsan men assaulting and robbing the few *Lixs giigyet* who ventured into the area.[24] At the time, the issues were attributed to the slackening of the regional economy, but the underlying causes were deeper. According to the Gitxsan, the *Lixs giigyet* were infringing on their trespass laws, first by not securing permission before entering the territories, and then by not offering payment to pass through the territories, or to ford rivers.

The accidental death of a young man at Hazelton while in the employ of A. C. Youmans, a merchant who had been doing business in the area for 10 years, brought to light the hostilities between the *Lixs giigyet* and the Gitxsan. Youmans was killed, according to Gitxsan law, after the accidental drowning of Billy Owen. Billy's father, *Haatq,* stabbed Youmans in public, and Youmans died a short while later.[25] Superintendent Henry Roycraft of the B. C. Provincial Police, the assigned magistrate, demanded that the person who "murdered Youmans" surrender. *Haatq* did so, against the wishes of the community. He admitted to stabbing Youmans, and said in his defence that it was his understanding that Youmans had had a hand in the death of his son, as he had kept the death secret for three days. *Haatq* was remanded for trial and sent to Victoria.[26]

The *Simgigyets* of the area wrote to Victoria arguing for clemency and urging the government to pardon *Haatq*, as he had only been following First Nations' law. They explained the "laws of the Kitiskseans," and outlined the possibility that Youmans could have had a hand in Billy Owen's death:

> If one Kitisksean A, asks another, B, either to work for him or to go hunting or fishing and that B should die from any cause while so employed, then A, when he arrives back at his village at once tells the relations of B and also gives the relations a present to show that he, A, had no bad feelings against B and that he does not want any bad feelings between B's relations and himself. If A does not tell about the death of B shortly after his return and is then supposed to have had a hand in the death of B then the relations will kill him for as [sic] they suppose he has killed their relations.[27]

The conviction and subsequent imprisonment of *Haatq* brought a further lobby by *Simgigyet Geddun-cal-doe*. *Simgigyet Geddun-cal-doe* repeated what other Gitxsan *Simgigyets* had said at *Haatq's* preliminary hearing — that Youmans' actions indicated guilt, and that *Haatq* was justified in taking his life. Attorney General John Robson responded that, though it may have been more prudent of Youmans to follow Indian custom, Gitxsan law was not binding on him, and it was the Queen's law by which all people were now governed.[28] The inference that Gitxsan law held little merit only exacerbated an already tense situation.

Another justifiable homicide, in the eyes of the Gitxsan, created such tensions in the area that the Gitxsan almost declared war on the *Lixs giigyet*. The dispute started with a shaman called *Neatsqu* who had claimed the right to the name *Hanamuq* at an earlier *yukw*, or feast; it ended with his death at the hands of *Hanamuq's* husband, *Kamalmuk*, also known as Kitwancool Jim, in February 1888.[29] *Kamalmuk* killed *Neatsqu* after the death of his two sons from measles, and went home to Kitwancool believing the issue was over. *Neatsqu's* family, however, wanted revenge, and the Rev. William Pierce was able to convince them to put the entire issue in the hands of the law.[30] The Kitwancool community felt that *Kamalmuk* was justified in killing *Neatsqu* and the subsequent death of *Kamalmuk* at the hands of the constable who had been sent to arrest him escalated tensions in the region.

The Gitxsan responded first by deferring to their own law, but after they had been threatened with armed confrontation, they placed the matter before Capt. Fitzstubbs, the appointed Magistrate for the District, hearkening back to the promise made after the 1872 fire at Gitsegukla. In restoring order, FitzStubbs invited the *Simgigyets* of Gitanmaax, Kitwangak, Gitsegukla, Kispiox, and Hagwilget to a meeting where he summarized the Queen's law. It was important to Fitzstubbs to outline the "terms in which they were to live in the future." This included a clear statement about how disputes were to be resolved, and an outline of what the law prohibited. Fitzstubbs stressed that it would be the *Simgigyets* who would bring the disputes forward, and that every person, high or low, was "bound by and protected by the law." The *Simgigyets* were presented with the choice: continue to operate under Gitxsan law, or face war.[31]

The Crown did not acknowledge the importance of Gitxsan law as it applied to unknown deaths. Knowledge of these matters, though understandably different from the common law, would have afforded the Crown a fuller understanding of Gitxsan law. A more substantive investigation at this time, and a broader debate of the Crown's position, would have revealed the root cause of the tensions in the region: the waning independence of the community, their disappearing land and resource base, and their forced inclusion in Canada without definable rights. According to Tomlinson, the Gitxsan claimed that the exclusive right "to hunt, fish and gather fruit in any particular place is an hereditary right enjoyed by us before the white man came among us. It is a right most vigorously upheld by all our tribes, without exception."[32] Unfortunately, Canada's only solution to resolving the conflict was the establishment of the Babine Indian Agency in 1889, mainly to keep the peace.[33]

The Land Question

Aside from the failure of the provincial and Dominion governments to ac-knowledge Gitxsan law, the Gitxsan were nervous that the government was sending more *Lixs giigyet* to steal their land. Until the early 1880s, newcom-ers appeared to be passing through, and rarely stayed around the forks of the Skeena, Bulkley, and Kispiox Rivers. The improvements to the district, the telegraph line and upgraded trails, spurred by discovery of gold at Lorne Creek and Omineca, brought a steadier traffic into the area. *Lixs giigyet* were becoming permanent residents; they were staking out homesteads, and com-peting for food and furs alongside the Gitxsan. The government was allowing this to occur without consultation with the community.

BC Colonial/Provincial Indian Land Policy: 1850–1875

The Oregon Boundary Treaty of 1846 consolidated British interests on the Northwest coast and provided what historian Richard Mackie called "the legitimate opportunity for the non-Native person to settle in British territory west of the Rockies."[34] A charter was granted to the Hudson's Bay Company on 13 January 1849 for the advancement of colonization and the encourage-ment of trade and commerce, and to clear indigenous title.[35] When the colonies of Vancouver Island and British Columbia merged in 1866, however, First Nations title questions were still unresolved, and serious flaws were ap-parent in the colonial Indian land and title policy.

Following the British colonial policy as reflected in the Royal Proclamation of 1763, the Hudson's Bay Company had secured 14 "cede and surrenders" around Fort Victoria and Port Rupert by 1854. These treaties purchased the title of the community, and laid out the rights of First Nations community members. The provisions were straightforward: the First Nations ceded their territories, expecting that they could continue with their fisheries as before, and continue to pursue their livelihood in areas the colony considered "uninhabitable" or "waste." First Nations community members were to have the same rights as the *Lixs giigyet*.[36] For the purpose of determining the extent of the communities' title and property rights, James Douglas viewed First Nations tenure in terms of their agricultural pursuits (as defined by the colonial administration), fishing stations, village sites, and cemeteries or sacred sites. Although the treaties were silent on community member's rights, Douglas's policy in general assumed that First Nations community members were to be granted the same rights as the settlers in such matters as business opportunities and the acquisition of lands adjacent to their communities. The land settlement policy ought to have accommodated the clearing of First Nations title according to prevailing British and North American standards; that is, through purchase.[37]

Although it had been well known since 1760 in British North America that the Crown compensated First Nations not only for their title to their settlements and gardens but also for their hunting grounds, the Crown remained ambivalent about the legal nature of First Nations title. The government convinced itself that lands and resources for the settlement of foreign populations and the acquisition of resource rights by third parties did not displace First Nations from their natural livelihood. West Coast First Nations were seen to derive their livelihood as fishers, hunters, or labourers, and these occupations were not seen as conflicting, as the newcomers preferred employment as farmers, miners, foresters, or industrialists. In the eyes of the Crown, Aboriginal people's livelihood did not require vast reserves. Indeed, in some areas the colonial government relied on arguments that denied First Nations' title to their territory as well as the ability to manage the lands in a beneficial manner.

"Some of the old Indians still maintain that the lands over which they formerly roamed and hunted are theirs by right," wrote Indian Agent William McKay in 1885. "I have met this claim by stating that as they have not fulfilled the divine command, 'to subdue the earth,' their pretensions to ownership, in this respect, are untenable."[38]

The annexation of First Nations land was justified on the basis that they did not use the land and resources effectively, and, hence, could not own them. The Crown again relied on the supposition that the pre-contact livelihood of First Nations could continue undisturbed, as they held property only in the products of their labour, and not in the territories that they habitually used. Further, since the Crown insisted that the Vancouver Island colony be self-sufficient, Douglas was unable to convince the House of Assembly to purchase First Nations title on either Vancouver Island after 1858 or on the mainland after 1862, or to allocate existing funds to purchase additional titles.[39] The debate continued in the Assembly, where Mr. Foster, the Member for Cowichan, raised the point that there was widespread belief among the colonists who were purchasing land that a portion of the money they paid was going toward securing First Nations' title. But the House felt it was the responsibility of the home government "to quiet the Indians" with respect to the title question, and concluded that the "quieting of those claims at this time would be a serious drawback to the improvements of the colony, taxing the resources of the Colony, making it unattractive to settlers."[40] The purchase of Indian lands ceased. This set up a series of logical inconsistencies: first, the colony disregarded British constitutional principles of securing title by purchasing the territory from the Aboriginal inhabitants before reselling it, leaving those lands open to future conflicts; and second, the colony shirked its responsibility to the settlers by permitting them to believe that a portion of the monies they were paying for the land was going toward such purchases, and the land itself was free from all covenants.

As a compromise, the colony continued to act on its modified Indian Policy, allocating only reserve land. All reserves set aside in British Columbia, on the island and on the mainland, were to include the First Nations' cultivated fields and village sites, as well as all lands that First Nations "invariably conceive a strong attachment to, and prize more." The "reserve only" policy was in keeping with James Douglas's goal of establishing "settlements of Natives" in order that they become civilized, Christian, and industrious.[41] He felt that, by establishing independent settlements, he was being fair to the state and looking out for the well-being of the Indians. He predicted that the First Nations of British Columbia would easily be assimilated into the surrounding communities, provided that they were first "placed under the proper moral and religious training, and left, under the protection of laws that would initially provide for their own maintenance and support."[42] Douglas's vision included the assumption that surplus lands would be leased, and over time the only First Nation people on the reserves would be the elderly and the infirm.

There was a surprising lack of information about First Nations livelihood pursuits, the content of their governance, and the substance of their title, and little was done to define either the reserves or lands identified as "special lands, cemeteries, or village sites" as having any significance to community members, or even being under their jurisdiction. As the anthropologist Wilson Duff points out, writing about the Douglas treaties, part of the problem was that the *Lixs giigyet* had little understanding of the nature of West Coast land tenure or governance structures. Duff suggests that, though James Douglas understood that the Songhees groups with whom he elected to treat were corporate groups, owning lands "exclusively" and with "definable boundaries," he neglected to investigate the nature of inter-family relationships, the use of "shared spaces" with respect to resources exploitation, and the widely dispersed seasonal sites to which the Songhees moved on an annual basis. Furthermore, though Douglas affirmed the "natural employment" of the Songhees was to be left undisturbed, he failed to integrate protection of these rights into the emerging body of law, as well as to acknowledge the community's "new rights" as subjects of the Crown.[43]

Douglas's "reserve only" policy was problematic, and though its goals were to provide the community with "homelands," and that, over time, community members would have the right to "pre-empt lands" adjacent to these villages according to colonial land policy, this was not the case. Surplus reserve lands not used by the community would be leased or sold, with the monies invested for the benefit of the community — i.e., to provide the necessary tutelage and cultural instruction in order that First Nations community members would become indistinguishable from the colonists.[44] It was anticipated that the community would choose their village sites, lands that they had under cultivation, cemeteries, locations that held special significance, and fishing sites. The policy anticipated that the average community would be allotted, on average, 10 acres per family of five. In practice, this amounted to less than five acres per family. The surveyors would arrive, ask an arbitrary set of members which lands were to be set aside for gardens, fishing stations, village sites, cemeteries, and ceremonial grounds, complete a cursory survey, and then leave, all in a matter of days.[45] Although the process of identifying reserves was initially and faithfully carried out, formal consultation with First Nations — the surveys, the gazetting, and public notification — lagged behind.[46]

By 1865, some reserves that had been at least surveyed were being, as the historian Robin Fisher describes it, "whittled down."[47] For example, Joseph Trutch, then Chief Commissioner of Lands and Works, was asked to make available to settlers lands that had been set aside for First Nations communities along the Thompson River. "The Indians," Trutch wrote, "have really no right to the lands they claim, nor are they of any actual value or utility to them; and I cannot see why they should either retain these lands to the prejudice of the general interests of the colony, or be allowed to make a market of them either to the Government or to individuals."[48]

Similarly, the Reserve Allocation Commission, while adjudicating a dispute over the re-allocation of reserve lands in the Kootenay region in 1887, said to Chief Isadore and the Kootenay First Nation, "You know that the white men come to this country and take up the land, according to its laws. There is a good deal of land the Indians do not use and do not require. It is the same in the Kootenay as in other places where there are Indians."[49]

Trutch's assumption that First Nations did not use the lands allotted to them according to European agricultural standards, and therefore did not deserve to have them, led to a general questioning of the size of existing reserves, especially those that had been surveyed but not gazetted. Questions then arose over the use of funds from lease or sales of reserve lands. This was contrary to Douglas's vision of the reserves and the use of funds, either from leases or sales. In Douglas's vision, the lands could become a "homeland" for the First Nations community, and monies garnered from sales or leases could be used to support education and pensions for community members. Trutch's policy, however, quickly developed into a denial of Aboriginal title and the arbitrary allocation of relatively small parcels of land which could be rescinded without compensation.[50] Douglas's compromise, inaugurated by 1856, was to set aside reserves according to the wishes of the particular Aboriginal community, and it met with the approval of most. However, as Fisher points out, it was when the subsequent governors, Kennedy and Seymour, permitted the erosion of the reserves after 1862 that the Land Question became the "Land Issue."[51]

The revisionist position of Joseph Trutch — that of reducing reserve lands, as well as selling unused portions of reserves — was particularly disturbing to First Nations. Their concerns centred, first, on title (i.e., compensation for the loss of access to the territories from which they elicited a traditional livelihood), and second, the process (being allocated a reserve, then having it either rescinded or a portion sold, without formal relations or consultation). Trutch's main argument for reducing the reserves was that their size was, for the most part, "disproportionate to the numbers and requirements of Indians residing in those Districts."[52] When faced with the justification of the reduction, as well as the cost, Trutch, instead of heeding the advice of his colleagues to purchase the surplus lands, elected to question the legality of the allocation policy in general, as there was "no written document on the matter in the Land Office."[53]

The issue of reserve allocation and the soundness of British Columbia's title were raised by Canada in talks with British Columbia before and after Confederation. In a letter to Prime Minister J. A. Macdonald on the eve of British Columbia's entry into Confederation, Trutch made it clear that the Indians, as special wards of the Crown, had lands set aside that were both proportionate and sufficient for their needs, and that the

> title of the Indians in fee of the public lands, or any portion of, therefore, has never been acknowledged by Government, but on the contrary, is strictly denied. In no case has any special agreement been made with any of the tribes of the Mainland for the extinction of their claims of possession; but these claims have been held to have been fully satisfied by securing for each tribe, as the progress of the settlement of the country seemed to require, the use of sufficient tracts of land for their wants for agriculture and pastoral purposes.[54]

During the Confederation debates of March 1870 in the British Columbia Legislature, however, there was some discussion of the Indian Question. One motion proposed the "protection of Indians during the change of government" (it was defeated 20 to 1), and another, that would have extended "Canadian Indian Policy to the Province," was withdrawn.[55] Clause 13 of the final Terms of Union was added in Ottawa, the drafting attributed to Trutch.[56] Although Clause 13 transfers the "charge of Indians to the Dominion," it states that "a policy as liberal as that hitherto pursued by the British Columbia Government shall be continued by the Dominion Government after the Union."[57] Canada was unaware that "liberal" treatment meant that it had been the practice of the local government to allocate only 10 acres per family of five. Canada's policy had been to allocate, at minimum, 80 acres per family of five, that the Dominion receive a formal surrender of all traditional lands, that the community have continued access to hunting, fishing, and trapping lands, an annuity assessed and given, and that "Indians and lands reserved for Indians" were to be administered under the *Indian Act*. After Confederation, it became apparent to David Laird, Canadian Minister for the Interior, that the framers of this clause "could hardly have been aware of the marked contrast between the Indian policies which had, up to that time, prevailed in Canada and British Columbia, respectively."[58] This prompted Trutch to write again to Macdonald:

> The Canadian system, as I understand it, will hardly work here. We have never bought out any Indian Claims to land, nor do they expect we should, but we reserve for their use and benefit from time to time tracts of sufficient extent to fulfill all their reasonable requirements for cultivation or grazing. If you now commence to buy Indian title to the lands of BC you would go back on all that has been done here for 30 years past and would be equitably bound to compensate the tribes who inhabited the districts now settled or farmed by white people equally with those in the more remote and uncultivated portions.[59]

It was apparent to the Dominion that the Indian Land Question was not going to be resolved easily. There were concerns and discussions going on about the state of Indian affairs in British Columbia, especially the failure to extinguish Indian title, and the report of the Justice Minister as to whether land laws enacted in British Columbia should be allowed or disallowed by the Dominion government. A strong argument was put forward to disallow or amend the *Land Act*, which affected Crown Lands in British Columbia, but, as Justice Minister Telesphore Fournier noted, the British Columbia Legislature had by "statute admitted Indian sovereignty to all lands of the Province," and since there were no formal surrenders, "the Indians" could claim title to the entire province. Fournier substantiated his statement by pointing out that "from the earliest times, England has always felt it imperative to meet the Indians in council, and to obtain surrender of tracts of Canada."

As Canada was unwilling to wade into the debate over the validity of British Columbia's claim to title, a compromise was proposed to organize a Reserve Allocation Commission to settle the Indian Land Question. Fournier concluded:

> Upon this assurance of the Government of British Columbia the undersigned recommends that the *Act* be left to its operation. Although the undersigned cannot concur in the view that the objections taken are entirely removed by the action referred to; and, though he is of opinion that, according to the determination of council upon the previous *Crown Lands Act*, there remains serious question as to whether the *Act* now under consideration is within the competence of the provincial

legislature, yet since, according to the information of the undersigned, the statute under consideration has been acted upon, and is being acted upon largely in British Columbia, and great inconvenience and confusion might result from its disallowance; and, considering that the condition of the question at issue between the two governments is very much improved since the date of his report, the undersigned is of opinion that it would be the better course to leave the *Act* to its operation.[60]

A three-man Indian Reserve Commission was set up by joint agreement of the governments of Canada and British Columbia. They directed their attention to the allocation of reserves in British Columbia, based on the formula of 20 acres per family of five. Fournier sensed that British Columbia was attempting to legislate with respect to public lands, as if those lands were its absolute property. As he observed, Article 109 of the *British North America Act, 1867,* conveyed public lands "subject to any trust existing thereof, and to any interest other than that of the province in the same,"[61] and this had been understood by the Dominion to be "some First Nations interest" in the public lands of the province. The significance of Fournier's argument, as far as First Nations were concerned, was that it was obvious that, until Aboriginal title was cleared, they held this interest.

According to the political scientist Paul Tennant, although Canada initially tried to manoeuvre British Columbia, after Confederation in 1871, into a more favourable First Nations policy, it became apparent by 1875 that the only compromise that could be reached would be with respect to reserve size, omitting the question of Aboriginal title throughout the traditional territory of any one of the First Nations.[62] Thus, by the turn of the century, the myth of unencumbered Crown title prevailed in the minds of the *Lixs giigyet* — a myth maintained through explicit provincial legislation that excluded the political voice of First Nations, and by the administration of federal Indian policy without clear "rights" set out for the communities.

The Establishment of the Reserve Commission in 1875

The Indian Reserve Commission was created in 1875, with a mandate to "visit with all convenient speed, in such order as may be found desirable, each Indian nation . . . in British Columbia and after a full inquiry on the spot . . . to fix and determine for each . . . the number and extent, and locality of the Reserve or reserves to be allowed to it."[63]

Initially, the commission was composed of three men: Archibald McKinley for the province, Alexander Anderson for the Dominion, and Gilbert Sproat, a joint appointment of both governments. Their mandate was to fix reserves according to the wishes of the community, with the allocated reserves being held in trust by the Dominion.[64] By 1877, the provincial government was complaining about the expense. In 1880, Peter O'Reilly was appointed sole commissioner. The Reserve Commission, in allocating lands, was to "have special regard to the habits, wants and pursuits of [Indians,] to assist [them] to raise themselves in the social and moral scale . . . encourage them in any branch of industry [and to ensure] an ample provision of water."[65]

The commission's first attempt to settle the Land Question on the north coast started earnestly in 1882, but O'Reilly was instructed only to survey reserves according to the prevailing standards — i.e., setting aside lands that community members felt strongly about, such as village sites, gardens, and cemeteries.[66] He ran into antagonism from the Nisga'a and the Tsimshian, Gitxsan neighbours, and was expelled from the area. This led to the Northwest Coast Royal Commission in 1886, at which the Nisga'a and the Tsimshian lobbied that "a treaty be made with them with reference to the land," "a sum paid down, or annual subsidies," or, in "lieu of payment," community members be allowed to choose land outside the reserves at "160 acres for each individual."[67] The Tsimshian and Nisga'a were clearly concerned with more than the loss of their lands; they feared a loss of freedom, were concerned about federal Indian administration, and wanted a treaty. The Royal Commission determined their demands to be unrealistic, however, and their concerns were only addressed in the form of the Reserve Commission re-visiting the region at a later time, and using existing information to set aside reserve lands.

The Reserve Commission did not reach Gitxsan territories until the 1890s, by which time it was generally known that the setting aside of reserves begged the question of title. When O'Reilly came to the Skeena, there was widespread Gitxsan opposition to any reserve allocation. The Gitxsan knew that the Nisga'a and Tsimshian had expelled the surveyors in 1882 because they feared that their lands and fishing stations would be taken from them. The Gitxsan were also aware of how the government had treated the Songhees people in Victoria, and were fearful that their reserve would also be given, then taken away.

Early Land Claims: 1884–1888

A Royal Commission conducted at Lorne Creek in late 1884 revealed that the concerns of the Gitx̱san were not really about incidental trespasses or the newcomers' inability to work with Gitx̱san law. It was about land, resources, and authority in their *lax'wiiyip*. The Gitx̱san petition requested government assistance to sort out the Land Question as they saw it. To the Gitx̱san, the district was theirs, the resources in it were theirs, and authority over the persons in it was theirs. The presence of the *Lixs giigyet* without clear relations was unsettling and incomprehensible. The *Simgigyets* argued:

> From time immemorial the limits of the district in which our hunting grounds are found have been well defined. This district extends from a rocky point called "Andemane" some two and a half or three miles from a village on the Skeena River to a creek called "She-quin-khatt," which empties into the Skeena below Lorne Creek. We claim the ground on both sides of the river, as well as the river within these limits, and as all our hunting territories, fruit gathering and fishing operations are carried out in this district, we truly say we are occupying it.
>
> The district is not held unitedly by all the members of the tribe but is portioned out among the several families, and no family has a right to trespass on another's grounds: so that if any family is hindered from hunting on their own ground, there is nowhere else for them to go — they lose all the benefits they derived from their hunting, as they cannot follow the animals across the bounds into their neighbour's grounds. We would liken this district to an animal, and our village, which is situated in it, to its heart. Lorne Creek, which may be likened to one of the animals [sic] feet, we feel that the white men, by occupying this creek, are, as it were, cutting off a foot. We know that an animal may live without one foot, or even both feet; but we also know that every such loss renders him more helpless, and we have no wish to remain inactive until we are almost or quite helpless. We have carefully abstained from molesting the white men during the past summer. We felt that though we were being wronged and robbed, but as we had not given you the time or opportunity to help us, it would not be right for us to take the matter into our own hands.

Now we bring the matter before you, and respectfully call upon you to prevent the inroads of any white men upon the land within the fore-mentioned district. In making this claim we would appeal to your sense of justice and right.[68]

The most significant point was that the district was "not held unitedly by all members of the tribe," but was "portioned out among the several families," and if "any one family is hindered on their own ground," they have no "right to trespass on another's land." The *Simgigyets* continued:

> We hold these lands by the best of all titles. We have received them as gifts from the God of Heaven to our forefathers, and we believe that we cannot be deprived of them by anything short of direct injustice. In conclusion, we would ask you, would it be right for our chiefs to give licence to members of the tribe to go to the district of Victoria to measure out, occupy and build upon lands in that district now held by white men, as grazing or pasture land? Would the white men now in possession permit it, even if we told them that, as we were going to make a more profitable use of the land, they had no right to interfere? Would the government permit it? If it would not be right for us so to act, how can it be right for the white men to act so to us?[69]

This claim was based on Gitxsan law and governance. The Gitxsan continued to press for recognition of their title, and wanted to come to an agreement with the Dominion that included the integration of their laws and governance in their *lax'wiiyip*. They argued that their rights were exclusive, that they could hunt, fish, or gather fruit in any particular place. They were

> hereditary rights enjoyed by us before the white man came among us. It is a right most rigorously upheld by all our tribes without exception. Our hunting and fruit gathering are the principal sources of our livelihood. Do away with them and we are at the mercy of the white man. We are prepared to maintain them in our own way or we are willing for the government to maintain them for us by law but we will not permit them to be interfered with.[70]

Reserve Allocations: 1891–1898

Regrettably, neither the federal nor the provincial authorities truly grasped the Gitxsan concerns. A clear response to this petition in 1884 might have sent future Land Question debates on a distinctly different trajectory. In theory, the allocation of reserves was insufficient to address Gitxsan concerns without a defined relationship and clearly articulated rights of access throughout their territories. The Reserve Only policy forwarded initially by the colony (and after Confederation by the province) and endorsed by the Dominion of Canada fell short of the expected adherence to British North American constitutional norms, where the Crown met First Nations in council to discuss terms of surrender, annuities, reserves, rights of access to traditional territories, and the subsequent relationship.

Reserve allocations, though delayed in Nisga'a territories, went ahead as scheduled around Gitxsan communities. In August 1891, Peter O'Reilly made a hasty survey trip and allotted reserves at Gitanamaax, Hagwilget, Moricetown, Babine Lake, Kispiox, Gitsegukla, and Gitwankga; he encountered opposition at Kispiox and Gitwankga. At Kispiox, community members wanted their entire traditional territories put aside. O'Reilly could not do this, but pointed out that they would have continued access to their berry-picking places, hunting grounds, and fishing stations. It was only when he convinced community members that they would not be confined to the reserve that he was able to go ahead with the survey, and most issues regarding questions of title quieted. During a second visit in 1893, surveyors met opposition at Gitwankga. The resident Indian Agent, R. E. Loring, mediated the dispute, and the surveyors continued with their work. For the most part, reserve allocation continued steadily from 1888 until 1900.

Gitxsan concerns, however, were not limited to the recognition of title. Rather, issues of trespass, the imposition of *Indian Act* strictures with respect to movement off reserve, the anti-Potlatch laws, and the sale or lease of reserve lands were the main considerations of the *Simgigyets*.

Antagonism toward the Potlatch among various newcomers throughout the province had been mounting in the years prior to the amendment of the *Indian Act* in 1884 that outlawed the ceremonial feast. The clergy had a list of reasons to ban the Potlatch, ranging from the "wanton destruction of property" to the "giving away of excessive amounts of property," and from the "eating of dogs" to the "fact that it promoted laziness" and indebtedness. There was a counter-lobby by other clergy, who argued that the Potlatch was similar to many Christian festivals. The legislation outlawing the Potlatch stipulated that, if convicted, hosts or participants would face imprisonment two to six months.

Enforcement of the Potlatch laws threatened Capt. Fitzstubbs's plan of indirect rule, and he agreed to let the Potlatch law "sleep for the winter."[71] R. E. Loring, his successor, was likewise unable to find reasonable arguments for why Potlatch participants should be arrested. He agreed with Fitzstubbs that, over time, the *yukw* would cease, and arresting Gitxsan people for holding the feast or attending it only courted resistance. The law was ambiguous, in any case; the Potlatch could arguably be a funeral feast or just a community social.[72] In fact, as Loring observed, the Gitxsan had already refrained from the offensive aspects of the feast, having curtailed the eating of dogs and the wanton distribution or destruction of property. As far as Loring was concerned, the *Yukw* by 1901 had disappeared; more accurately, it had been modified. However, as long as the community kept the peace and acted with discretion, Loring was satisfied to ignore Gitxsan ritual life. He was kept busy settling fishing disputes and ensuring that community members had enough wood and food for the winters. Besides this routine business, his reports are filled with the continued allocation of reserves and the dispensing of relief.[73]

The Gitxsan now realized that the *Lixs giigyet* were not just passing through. They were fencing off sections of the *lax'wiiyip* for agricultural pursuits, and by 1896 had become the majority in the area.

The Stewart-Vowell Commission

In 1910 the Gitxsan sent a petition to Prime Minister Sir Wilfrid Laurier, asking that their lands be reinstated, their system of administration returned, that they be taken out from under the *Indian Act*, and to be free under the British flag. The years just prior to this saw the *Lixs giigyet* migrating into the Upper Skeena. The construction of the Grand Trunk Pacific Railway created new markets and provided access to outside markets, stimulating the agricultural, mining, and forestry industries. Though preferring the Bulkley Valley in Wet'suwet'en territory, the *Lixs giigyet* made their way into the Kispiox and Kitwanga Valleys. These moves alarmed the Kispiox and Kitwancool communities, and raised again the land title question. From contacts at the coast, the Gitxsan were able to join with the larger provincial land claims movement that sought, through lobbying Ottawa and by other legal means, to get acknowledgement of Aboriginal title. First Nations were seeking compensation for territories that had been alienated; they wanted explicit rights for hunting, fishing, and trapping, citizenship rights, and recognition of their right to self-government. Issues around the Hazelton-Kispiox area came to a head in 1908 when a series of conflicts arose in Gitx̱san, Gitanyow, and Wet'suwet'en communities over continued *Lixs giigyet* inroads. The Department of Indian Affairs promised an inquiry.

At meetings in Hazelton on July 18 and 19, 1909, Special Commissioners Stewart and Vowell, appointed by the Department of Indian Affairs, listened to Gitx̱san grievances.[74] Although nothing concrete materialized from the meetings, the Gitx̱san sentiments about the Land Question crystallized. They claimed the right to occupy and administer their territory according to their laws and customs, asserting that *Simgigyets* were the owners of the lands — "the lands of their forefathers." Thus, for the Gitx̱san, there was "no vacant or un-owned land" in their *lax'wiiyip*, for "the sum of the territories owned by each *Simgigyets* equaled the entire Gitx̱san territory."[75] They contended that the current reserve system was against their traditional ways, and, as the land had neither been taken from them by conquest nor been purchased, they laid claim to the entire region.

The only response the government could muster was to continue the survey of reserves. It also sent the Rev. J. McDougall to the Skeena River to consult with the communities about their grievances, and to ensure that the *Lixs giigyet* had not, and would not, encroach on the community's reserve lands.

Grievances were similar throughout the territories. "The Government has never done anything for us," the Gitx̱san claimed. "The land belongs to us. We are living in hope day by day that the Government will do us right."[76]

"Take the reserves and the *Indian Act* and let us die in peace," they said. "Give us back the right which was ours. Deer, fish, fruit, and liberty. The strong man has done us wrong. We ask the Government to do for us what is fair and right."[77]

Once again the community wanted their historic title acknowledged. They also wanted the franchise, for they realized that being disenfranchised meant that they did not have a voice in regional matters. McDougall's recommendation was that the federal and provincial governments secure the "extinguishment of the Indian title to the lands in British Columbia."[78]

In 1907 the Province of British Columbia, through a Minute-in-Council, gave notice to the federal government regarding two areas of disagreement over the allocation of reserves. The province argued that some reserves were too large, and that the reversionary interest in the reserve lands was vested in the province.[79] The province then launched legal proceedings in the BC Supreme Court, laying claim to lands that First Nations had abandoned, and seeking the disposition of the resources on the reserves in general. Though the case was dropped in the province in order to be taken to the Supreme Court of Canada, and then dropped altogether in favour of negotiations, it was apparent that the province laid claim to the reserve lands. The federal government sought a judicial inquiry into the province's claim of undisputed title. Representatives of Canada and British Columbia drew up a list of 10 questions, the first three having to do with Aboriginal title, the remaining seven concerned with the size of reserves, reserve resources such as minerals and timber, and the claim of the province on abandoned reserve lands.

This judicial action was brought to a halt when BC Premier Richard McBride categorically refused to endorse the first three questions. British Columbia claimed that the title held by First Nations was limited to "use and occupancy," and, under Clause 13 of the Terms of Union, the Dominion held no "beneficial interest in such lands" as guardian of First Nations. Moreover, British Columbia argued, whenever the First Nation right to any reserve lands became extinguished by surrender, cessation of use, or occupancy, the lands reverted to the Province.[80] The Province sought to formalize the revisionism policy of Trutch.

The McKenna-McBride Commission: 1912–1916

The Dominion was nervous about the unfinished nature of the allocation of reserves, and the provincial claim to the ceded lands. Though the *Indian Act* had been amended to reflect the Dominion's position, the federal government negotiated the McKenna-McBride Agreement of September 24, 1912, establishing the Royal Commission on Indian Affairs in British Columbia and laying out its terms of reference. The McKenna-McBride Commission, as it became known, was established solely to resolve the issues of reserve acreage, underlying title, and reversionary interests.

Initially, the size and location of the reserves were to be set, and, if any of them were found to be too large, unused portions were to be sold, the proceeds split between the province and the Department of Indian Affairs. Should new reserves or additional lands be required, the province was to take all necessary steps to locally reserve additional lands. After the reserves were determined, to the satisfaction of all five commissioners, the reserve lands were to be conveyed by the province to the Dominion. The commission, over the next three years, recommended the creation of 482 new reserves, and "cut off" a total of 47,058 acres from existing reserves.[81]

The formation of the commission prompted a well-organized response from British Columbia First Nations, who had organized around the Indian Rights Association.[82] In a circular letter sent throughout the province in December 1912, the association critiqued the mandate of the McKenna-McBride Agreement and the future Commission. They pointed out that the main question, that of title, was not included.[83]

As members of the Indian Rights Association, the Gitxsan were prepared to use the platform of the commission to raise their concerns over title. When the commission arrived to determine whether the reserves were adequate, Gitxsan representatives reiterated the position they had taken in the petition they had sent to Sir Wilfrid Laurier in 1910. The chairman's response was that they were there to "fix reserves," and the question of title or rights was not going to be discussed.[84] The commission's sole responsibility was to set the acreage of reserves, settle the question whether the province or Canada held title to the reserve lands, and determine whether it was the province or the First Nations community, through the federal government, that administered the trusts set up from the sale or lease of lands and the sale of resources or royalties.

In the end, it was determined that Canada held title to the reserves, and would provide the community with benefits from the sale or lease of reserve lands or resources. The Gitxsan, like other BC First Nations, rejected the findings of the McKenna-McBride Commission that either enlarged or reduced the reserves. As far as the Gitxsan were concerned, the issues of underlying title, control over trusts, and their personal legal status were questions that still needed to be addressed.

In 1919, the Tsimshian, the Nisga'a, and the Gitxsan issued a statement under the umbrella of the United Tribes of Northern British Columbia:

> That from time immemorial these tribes of Indians have been in the undisputed possession of the land of the northern part of the Province. We have lived and hunted upon it, fished in the streams that run on it, harvested the berries and fruits, built our houses and made our wood fire from its timber, and our forefathers are buried underneath its soil. It has been handed down to us from uncle to nephew from time immemorial to this present time.
>
> We do not understand how it is that the White men, men of intelligence who understand the laws of property, spend their time, labour

and money in trying to deny our claims and trying to make us believe that we have no right to the land. Practically throughout the rest of Canada tribal ownership has been fully acknowledged, and all dealings with the various tribes have been based upon the Indian Title so acknowledged.[85]

The three nations outlined their conditions for a settlement: they wanted to sit in Council with the Dominion, as outlined by the Royal Proclamation of 1763, and they required a voice in setting the conditions of the surrender; they wanted to control the monies from the sale or lease of lands, resources, or royalties; they stipulated that the communities in question be consulted prior to any reduction or cutoff of their reserves; they sought to have all foreshore, tidal or inland, included in the reserves to which they were connected in order that they could have full and permanent benefit related to their fisheries; they desired that their Indian title and rights be fully recognized by both the provincial and Dominion governments by either concession or through a judicial ruling, supported by an Act of Parliament.

An effort was made to present these concerns to the Joint Parliamentary and Senate Committee on Aboriginal Issues in 1927, but the Joint Committee ruled that all Aboriginal title issues were closed. First Nations had accepted additional reserve lands in 1916, and the Dominion had faithfully spent money and would continue to act on improvements to reserve communities, including medical care, education, and relief. Further, as all First Nations retained the right to hunt, gather, or fish in unoccupied provincial Crown lands, the federal government concluded that it had satisfied its obligations.[86] The only real action that the committee took was to recommend amendments to the *Indian Act*, which initially prevented non-Aboriginal persons from "raising funds to forward claims," later disallowing First Nations people to put forward claims against the Dominion, without first obtaining the permission of the Superintendent.[87] The modifications to the *Indian Act*, as well as the government's refusal to reimburse the petitioners for monies spent on legal counsel, effectively prevented First Nation headway on the land title issues until 1960.

CHAPTER THREE

The Trials of the Gitxsan

Delgam'Uukw v. *Attorney General of British Columbia*

IN 1884 THE GITXSAN ARGUED THAT THE RESERVE SYSTEM WAS AKIN TO LAMING an animal: the animal might live, but the quality of its life diminishes as it loses one of it its feet, then another, then a limb, and so on until it is unable to fend for itself. The practice of using the *lax'wiiyp* for subsistence and ceremonial purposes under provincial and federal management had weakened the Gitxsan's ability to derive a livelihood, as well as meet their social and ceremonial obligations. It was the goal of the Gitxsan when they filed their claim against the province on October 24, 1984, to argue that their *ayooks* and governance had a place in contemporary Canadian society, and that their *Ayooks* of *Naa hlimoot'* (laws of sharing) and traditional management regimes warranted respect and recognition. The Gitxsan believed that their Aboriginal and title rights to their *lax'wiiyip* existed until they formally surrendered them to the Crown. They believed, too, that the ensuing treaty relationship could start from the respectful position of integrating their *Ayooks* of *Naa hlimoot'* and related governance structures with provincial and federal legislation. The Gitxsan fully acknowledged the presence of the *Lixs giigyet* and their desire to live in the area, but they also believed that the Crown has an obligation to them as Indigenous people to protect their resources, including forestry, mineral resources, oil, and gas. When the Gitxsan filed suit against the province, they had exhausted all other avenues for negotiation. In the opening statement of the Plaintiffs, *Simgigyets Delgam'Uukw* and *Gisday Wa* asserted:

> Officials who are not accountable to this land, its laws or its owners have attempted to displace our laws with legislation and regulations. The politicians have consciously blocked each path within their system

that we take to assert our title. The courts, until perhaps now, have similarly denied our existence. In our legal system, how will you deal with the idea that the Chiefs own the land? The attempts to quash our laws and extinguish our system have been unsuccessful. *Gisday Wa* has not been extinguished.

If the Canadian legal system has not recognized our ownership and jurisdiction but at the same time not extinguished it, what has been done with it? Judges and legislators have taken the reality of Aboriginal title, as we know it, and tried to wrap it in something called Aboriginal rights. An Aboriginal rights package can be put on the shelf to be forgotten or to be endlessly debated at Constitutional Conferences. We are not interested in asserting Aboriginal rights. We are here to discuss territory and authority. When this case ends and the package has been unwrapped, it will have to be our ownership and our jurisdiction under our law that is on the table.[1]

A total of 35 Gitxsan and 13 Wet'suwet'en *Simgigyet and Sigidim haanak'a* filed suit against the Attorney General of British Columbia, arguing that, as they had not surrendered ownership and jurisdiction over the *lax'wiiyip,* they governed themselves according to the *ayooks* as laid down in the *adawaaks*. As far as the Gitxsan were concerned, title and authority over their *lax'wiiyip* had not been extinguished. They asked the court to define their legal rights in terms of ownership and jurisdiction, enabling the *Simgigyet* and *Sigidim haanak'a* to negotiate a treaty placing this ownership and jurisdiction in the context of Canada. For the Gitxsan, the purpose of the litigation from 1984 until the Supreme Court ruling in 1997 was to find a place for Gitxsan *Ayooks* of *Naa hlimoot'* in Canada, to legitimize their governance, to participate in resource management, and authorize access up to their territorial boundaries.

The *Delgam'Uukw* litigation is an integral part of the Gitxsan struggle to integrate their ownership and jurisdiction over land and authority through political negotiation and the Canadian courts. At trial, the *Simgigyet* and *Sigidim haanak'a* argued that their Aboriginal rights included the right to govern their traditional territories for themselves and their house members according to their laws, their political alliances, their legal code, and through their social institution of the feast. They argued that their rights included the right to ratify or refuse land titles or grants issued by the Province of British Columbia as of October 24, 1984, and claimed damages for the loss of all lands and resources transferred to third parties since the establishment of the colony in 1862. The Province of British Columbia counterclaimed that the plaintiffs had no right, title, or interest in and to the disputed territory and its resources, and that the plaintiffs' cause of action with respect to their Aboriginal title, right, or interest in and to the territory was solely for compensation from Canada.

The Gitxsan position has remained constant since the assertion of Crown sovereignty, in that they hold title until it is formally ceded to the federal Crown. In terms of reconciliation of their Aboriginal rights and title with that of the Crown, they desire access and management rights to their entire *lax'wiiyip*. As to the right to self-government, they anticipate that it will be based on the principles of the *Gim litxwid* (the governing body of the Gitxsan hereditary chiefs, appointed traditionally and recognized by the *huwilp*) contained in the *adawaaks* and their *ayooks*.

After 1927: Background to the 1987 Trial

Amendments to the *Indian Act* in 1927 effectively silenced First Nations across the country with respect to land title claims, but the grievances did not disappear. By 1927 it was apparent to both British Columbia First Nations and Canada that an impasse had been reached with respect to the BC Land Question and underlying title issues. Indeed, with the conclusion of Treaty 11 and its adhesion in 1921 and 1922, respectively, it was generally accepted that treaty-making in Canada had come to an end. By the end of the 1920s there remained vast regions of the nation where formal surrenders had not taken place and treaties had not been signed. Northern Quebec, Labrador, parts of the Northwest Territories, the Yukon, and most of British Columbia fell into this category. Canada in 1927 argued that it had fulfilled its obligations to British Columbia First Nations, irrespective of the due process of negotiating treaties and surrenders. Canada contended that British Columbia First Nations were treated in the same manner as other Aboriginal communities who held treaties. In other words, Canada provided annuities, monies for land either surrendered or leased from the communities' reserve lands, as well as benefits such as medicines, housing, education, and relief, and applied the state's enfranchisement policy to British Columbian First Nations accordingly. In addition, Canada argued that land rights in British Columbia had been met and fulfilled during the McKenna-McBride Commission of 1913-1916.

It was not until after World War II that these concerns re-surfaced. Though the 1951 *Indian Act* revisions quietly swept away the more offensive aspects of the legislation, such as the Potlatch prohibitions and the necessity of obtaining the permission of the Superintendent of Indian Affairs to enter into a claims process, the more specific concerns of First Nations people across the country — control over membership, culture, trusts, enfranchisement, education, and revenues from surrenders or leases — were not addressed.

First Nations leaders across the country were under the impression that these concerns would be addressed after the release of the Hawthorne Report in 1966[2] and in the reorganization of Indian Affairs in 1969. However, instead of complying with treaty obligations and addressing the land title question, in 1969 the federal government responded with a White Paper which stated that treaties were "an anomaly which should be reviewed to see how they could be equitably ended."[3] The White Paper recommended that jurisdiction over Indians should be transferred to the provinces, that reserve lands be granted to band members in fee simple, and that annuities be distributed among individual band members. Simultaneously, the federal government made a commitment to settle past grievances, based on the treaty relationship; although the government wanted to divest itself of "Indians and Indian lands," it was willing to act on its lawful obligations when it came to past grievances regarding the sale or lease of reserve lands, the issue of cut-off lands in British Columbia as a result of the McKenna-McBride Commission, and fraud with respect to the acquisition or disposal of reserve lands by employees or agents of the federal government.[4] Regarding Aboriginal title claims, the government determined that these concerns were "too vague" to be capable of a specific remedy. First Nations were faced with the prospect of having their reserve lands divided up and the *Indian Act* dissolved. In the areas where First Nations held treaties, it appeared that the cede and surrender agreements the communities had entered into in exchange for "lands set aside for their use and benefit" and "protection" were now being disregarded. For communities who had yet to formally cede their territories to the Crown, it appeared that their grievances were to continue to be ignored.

One effect of the White Paper was that it galvanized many First Nations organizations, including the National Indian Brotherhood, into lobbying for the recognition of Aboriginal rights. The White Paper was shelved, and there was little more debate until the Nisga'a took their claim to the Supreme Court in 1973 and First Nations' voices entered into the national political arena.

The *Calder* Case

In an attempt to resurrect their assertion of Aboriginal title in the Nass Valley, the Nisga'a in 1967 argued before the BC courts that Aboriginal title was recognized at common law and that the Nisga'a could satisfy the requirements of establishing it. Their goal was to obtain a declaration of their rights within traditional territory in order to negotiate a treaty. They did not claim that they were able to sell or alienate their right to possession, except to the Crown. They did, however, challenge the authority of British Columbia to make grants in derogation of their rights. Justice Hall in the Supreme Court of Canada set out the contours of the Nisga'a argument:

> The appellants rely on the presumption that the British Crown intended to respect Native rights; therefore, when the Nishga people came under British sovereignty they were entitled to assert, as a legal right, their Indian title. It being a legal right, it could not thereafter be extinguished except by surrender to the Crown or by competent legislative authority, and then only by specific legislation. There was no surrender by the Nishgas and neither the Colony of British Columbia nor the Province after Confederation, enacted legislation specifically purporting to extinguish the Indian title nor did Parliament at Ottawa.[5]

The Supreme Court decision was split: three judges held that the Nisga'a retained unextinguished title, three held that whatever title the Nisga'a had held was extinguished, and the seventh dismissed the claim on the grounds that the Nisga'a had failed to obtain a *fiat* from British Columbia to proceed with the litigation, and, as the case was dismissed on a technicality, the Court did not address the content of Aboriginal title. Six judges agreed that Aboriginal title could arise at common law without legislative recognition, based on colonial constitutional principles that the sovereign ought to recognize the property rights of the inhabitants upon acquisition of a new territory.

While the Supreme Court's ruling was inconclusive, the *Calder* decision made it clear that Aboriginal title was alive as a legal concept, despite the government's denial of it. Besides the *Calder* action, in the 1973 *Re Paulette* case, 16 chiefs were successful in registering a caveat on the title to approximately 700,000 square kilometres in the North West Territories, based on the claim that they had never ceded their Aboriginal rights to the

Crown.[6] Also in 1973, the James Bay Cree obtained an injunction to halt the construction of a hydro-electric dam at James Bay.[7] Though the injunction was nullified by the Court of Appeal, this action heralded the first modern treaty two years later in 1975.[8]

1973 was a year of change in law, policy, and attitude toward First Nation grievances, especially for communities that had not formally ceded their territories to the Crown. After the *Calder* case, the federal government conceded that its 1969 position was deficient, and responded with a comprehensive claims policy in August 1973. Cabinet agreed that there were two types of claims, specific and comprehensive, and that comprehensive claims were based on the traditional use and occupancy of land in areas where First Nation interests had yet to be extinguished by treaty or superseded by law. These claims were to be settled not only in cash, but with additional lands.

The federal government's subsequent policy of 1977, affirmed in 1981, stipulated that the community's Aboriginal title was to be ceded in exchange for a modified title (reserve lands), user rights within the traditional territory, and compensation.[9] It is generally accepted that, since August 1973, with respect to land and rights not formally ceded to the Crown, the federal government seeks to "signify the Government's recognition and acceptance of its continuing responsibility under the *British North America Act* for Indians and Lands Reserved for Indians," which it regarded as "an historic evolution dating back to the Royal Proclamation of 1763, which, whatever differences there may be about its judicial interpretation, stands as a basic declaration of the Indian people's interests in land in this country."[10] This change in policy also expressed the government's willingness to negotiate claims of Aboriginal title, especially in British Columbia, Northern Quebec, and the North West Territories on the basis "that where their traditional interest can be established, an agreed-upon form of compensation or benefit will be provided to Native people in return for their interest."[11]

In November 1977, there was renewed hope that the provincial and federal governments would sit down with the Gitxsan to negotiate a treaty. The treaty the Gitxsan were anxious to negotiate, however, was not based on the model that the James Bay Cree and Northern Inuit had just signed, but one that reflected Gitxsan jurisdiction throughout the territories in partnership with British Columbia, and protected by Canada. In a 1977 Declaration, the Gitxsan stated:

Since time immemorial, we, the Gitksan and Carrier People of the Kit-wanga, Gitanmaax, Shikadoak, Kispiox, Hagwilget and Moricetown, have exercised Sovereignty over our land. We have used and conserved the resources of our land, with care and respect. We have governed ourselves. We have governed the land, the waters, the fish and the animals. This is written on our totem poles. It is recounted in our songs and dances. It is present in our language and in our spiritual beliefs. Our Sovereignty is our Culture.[12]

Canada's Position

In 1978, the federal comprehensive land claims position was a joint process that included provincial governments. Though the particulars were yet to be fully developed, the federal government had made a commitment to negotiate comprehensive claims based on an inherent rights perspective — i.e., continuing use and occupancy of traditional lands where First Nations had Aboriginal interests that had not been relinquished by treaty or special legislation.

The federal position was uncomplicated: the government was willing to negotiate with First Nations on a variety of protection issues, such as hunting, fishing, and trapping, land title, compensation, and other rights and benefits in exchange for a release of their general and undefined Aboriginal title according to "past usage of the Crown." Thus, the First Nation was expected to cede its rights to its traditional territories in exchange for a set of user rights throughout their entire territories, demarcated reserved boundaries, and a set of conditions in which the government could infringe on the reserve lands and areas that held special significance.

The federal Crown was unwilling to entertain a model of self-government that reflected sovereignty, but it would consider an expanded role for band councils, transferring additional responsibilities for the management of services such as health, language, and culture to the community. While recognizing traditions and culture, the federal government expected greater accountability from the community. Self-government powers were limited to village concerns and the management of resources in the land claim area, excluding oil and gas. The federal Crown, however, understood the underlying difficulties the Gitxsan faced from provincial opposition to any governance model based on the hereditary office of the *Simgigyet* and *Sigidim haanak'a*, and integrating their *ayooks* with provincial ministerial authority. It was also apparent that the federal Crown, though interested in the "inherent rights" model for solving the land and governance questions, shied away from any direct intervention on behalf of the Gitxsan.

British Columbia's Position

British Columbia was willing to sit at the negotiating table as an observer in 1977, but the province was unwilling to "recognize the existence of an unextinguished Aboriginal title to land in the Province, nor does it recognize claims relating to Aboriginal title which give rise to other interest in lands based on traditional use and occupation of land."[13] The province was prepared to discuss the areas related to the harvesting of game or fur-bearing animals, joint management protocols with respect to future resource development, environmental protection, economic development, delivery of services, and the protection of First Nations culture. Moreover, if additional reserve lands were necessary, the province would entertain "selling the land to the federal government," only if it was determined that such sales would not be detrimental to provincial management, or that the loss of control over lands and resources for the benefit of all residents of British Columbia would not be affected. At this time, however, the province would not discuss matters that Aboriginal peoples maintained endowed them with additional benefits associated with their historic or current status as indigenous people, or as what the Hawthorne Report defined as "Citizens Plus."[14] Generally Citizens Plus rights are associated with First Nations' inherent right of access to unsettled lands for hunting, fishing, and trapping for subsistence, ceremonial and social purposes, and to some form of self-government limited to reserve lands. British Columbia's position was that the communities would have to relinquish their tax-free status and adopt a municipal-style form of self-government if Citizens Plus issues were broached.

The Gitxsan Position

In response to both the federal and provincial positions the Gitxsan initially sought to negotiate, first, a "blanket trap-line license" from the provincial government, and second, an opportunity to re-claim their inland salmon fishery. As they had co-existed with the animals and salmon for thousands of years, the Gitxsan believed they had not only the right to manage these resources but that it was in the best interests of the animals and the environment that they do so. They wanted control over what species were trapped and in what numbers, and proposed that each *wilp* be responsible for the areas within their *lax'wiiyip*, contrary to provincial requirements that neither respected *wilp lax'wiiyip* boundaries nor their rules of inheritance.

In the management of the fishery, the Gitxsan made efforts to resolve the conflict between the Department of Fisheries and Oceans and the traditional authority of the *Simgigyet* and *Sigidim haanak'a* over allocations and the scheduling of openings. The Gitxsan believe they ought be able to fish and process their catch where they live. *Simgigyet Ax Gwin Desxw* described these efforts at reconciliation:

> We wanted to develop an inland fishery that resembled our traditional one, so we wanted our people to be able to use, buy, sell, trade or barter fish caught on the Skeena in accordance to our traditional laws and customs.
>
> We wanted to reclaim the fishery that belongs to the hereditary chiefs. There are houses that own specific fishing stations or holes, sites, and the plan was that each household would use their own site or station. We wanted the chiefs to be the ones that would be in authority over the inland commercial fishery, so that house members would get some economic benefit from the inland fishery. . . .
>
> We want to work with other user groups, other native groups up and down the Skeena. We also want to meet with the commercial fishermen on the coast, and also the sport fishermen. We want to try and work out an arrangement of how we could all work together on the fishery on the Skeena River.
>
> The salmon are a real part of our lives. The Gitksan and Wet'suwet'en peoples are not going to leave where they live to fish, and we want to ensure that the resource is protected, we want to sustain the resource, we want to protect it for the future. We want to make sure that sawmills and logging companies do not have a negative impact on the habitat around the river or spawning beds.[15]

The Gitxsan also wanted a say in environmental standards when it came to forestry management. The *Simgigyet* and *Sigidim haanak'a* believed that the newcomer forest practices were making their ability to use the *lax'wiiyip* for subsistence impossible. As *Tenmigyet* testified, "You will not see moose standing in the middle of a clear-cut because they would not find anything to eat there. The same goes for the ground hogs, the martens, and even the mushrooms or our berries will never grow in a clear-cut."[16]

These negotiations, however, concluded almost as soon as they started. The Gitxsan had very little choice but to consider litigation, as they were unwilling to accept a treaty that required them, first, to cede and surrender their territories, and second, acquire a list of rights subject to Crown regulation. If they were to be a party to this treaty model, they believed, they would be required to compromise their traditional governance methods, limit their livelihood ventures to only a proportion of their *lax'wiiyip*, and modify their *ayooks* with respect to hunting, fishing, and berry-picking locations in light of Crown legislation and third party use, without adequate consultation or compensation.

When the *Lixs giigyet* arrived in the territories *circa* 1825 to trade, the Gitxsan remained independent, maintaining their own laws. They knew as early as 1884 that the loss of use of *lax'wiiyip* undermined their means of livelihood. They also knew that retaining authority in their territories was important for respectful relationships among themselves and the animals. Adherence to the laws of trespass and the ability to shoulder responsibility for respectful relations were obligations placed on all who came to the territories, according to Gitxsan *ayooks*.

The *Lixs giigyet* initially respected the laws of the Gitxsan, but after 1872 the situation changed. Issues regarding trespasses and the inability of the *Lixs giigyet* to respect the laws that governed a person's conduct in light of trespass or accidental death created tensions between Gitxsan communities and the local authorities. The unwillingness of the government to analyze the situation regarding trespass and homicide in the early 1880s created a sea of distrust that persists to this day. Similarly, early provincial insistence on allocating reserves without addressing the interrelationship between Aboriginal title, self-government, continued livelihood, and the harmonization of laws and jurisdiction, has not favoured respectful relations.

In 1910, the Gitxsan crystallized their position regarding the Land Question. They believed the *Lixs giigyet* were trespassing on their territories and ignoring their laws. The Gitxsan, like other British Columbian First Nations, knew they had land and social rights that rested in Imperial colonial law and practice. They maintained that their ownership, property rights, and administrative responsibilities persisted until they entered into formal surrenders. In the past, the Gitxsan had modified their laws with respect to capital crimes such as larceny and the various definitions of homicide. They had also acknowledged the sovereignty of the Crown. Moreover, James Douglas, at the time of declared sovereignty, knew that First Nations held "distinct ideas of property in land" and recognized their exclusive possessory rights.[17] After the Allied Tribes of British Columbia's failed attempt at litigation in 1910, the Nisga'a Petition of 1916, the United Tribes statement in 1919, and the Special Joint Senate Parliamentary Committee in 1927, the Gitxsan maintained that the issues of title, annuities, and citizenship were still unfinished business. These issues have remained the Gitxsan focus.

Delgam'Uukw v. *the Attorney General of British Columbia,* 1991[18]

Spurred by the lack of movement at the treaty table in the late 1970s and an inability to negotiate any substantive relationship with either the federal or provincial Crown, the Gitxsan elected to pursue the matter through the courts. They filed suit against the Attorney General of British Columbia on October 24, 1984. The trial lasted from 1987 to 1990, during which time the British Columbia Supreme Court was asked to rule on the legitimacy of Gitxsan ownership and jurisdiction that would enable the Gitxsan, through treaty, to place this ownership and jurisdiction in the context of Canada. *Simgigyet* and *Sigidim haanak'a,* in their 1984 pleadings, admitted that the underlying title to the soil of the territory, as outlined in their statement of claim, was in the Crown in right of British Columbia, but they argued that their Aboriginal title and rights entitled them to occupy and possess their individual *wilp* territories. As to Aboriginal title, the Gitxsan and Wet'suwet'en acknowledged they could not alienate their lands by sale, transfer, mortgage, or other dispossession except to Canada, in accordance with the requirements of the Royal Proclamation of 1763. The *Simgigyet and Sigidim haanak'a* sought to establish that they continued to be an organized society with a common language, traditions, and culture that were similar in all important respects to those of their ancestors. Consequently, they led their evidence in their own language, presented their customs, told their *adawaaks,* and explained their *ayooks* in order to confirm their own position as well as the findings of the experts who gave evidence in the areas of anthropology, archaeology, linguistics, history, geology, and fisheries.

The Gitxsan believed they met the four requirements of the *Baker Lake* test in which Federal Court of Canada identified the criteria for establishing Aboriginal title as an organized society.[19] The Gitxsan presented evidence that they and their ancestors were members of an organized society, that their society occupied the specific territory over which they asserted Aboriginal title, that this occupation was exclusive, and that these things were established facts at the time Great Britain asserted sovereignty.

During the course of the trial in the British Columbia Supreme Court, 1987 to 1991, the Gitxsan opened their *gelenk* (treasure boxes) and told the court how they had originally lived in the territories of the Skeena-Bulkley-Kispiox watersheds, had been expelled, and subsequently migrated back. The *Simgigyet* and *Sigidim haanak'a* told the court how they held authority contingent on adherence to their *ayooks,* which included stewardship toward the land and animals, as well as the ability to provide a livelihood for their *wilp* members. They maintained that they had not relinquished title to their territories, and that their jurisdiction and authority ought to encompass their entire *lax'wiiyip*, and not be limited to current reserve lands. In essence, although they conceded that sovereignty was held by the Crown, as an Indigenous people they were an integral aspect of Crown authority, and their rights in the region superseded those of the *Lixs giigyet.*

The judgement handed down in 1991 by Chief Justice McEachern fell short of their expectations. McEachern only saw the trial as "political," "about vast forest reserves," in a "vast emptiness" in northwest British Columbia.[20] He was able to conclude only that Gitxsan Aboriginal interests in the territory had been lawfully extinguished by the Crown during the colonial period, and non-reserve Crown lands, titles, and tenures granted by the Crown since the creation of the colony were unencumbered by any claim of Aboriginal title.[21] He referenced *Calder*[22] as evidence of the extinguishment of Aboriginal title and relied on the previous case as "clear and intentional extinguishment" of Gitxsan Aboriginal interest to their *lax'wiiyip* outside their villages and reserves. However, McEachern did determine that the Gitxsan, Wet'suwet'en, and Gitanyow were entitled to a declaration that they could use vacant Crown lands within the territories for Aboriginal sustenance pursuits, subject to provincial law and federal regulations.[23]

The Chief Justice, in essence, affirmed the traditional stance of British Columbia toward Aboriginal title, and mused that Gitxsan life, either currently or historically, was "far from stable and it stretches credulity to believe that remote ancestors considered themselves bound to specific lands."[24] He felt, moreover, that this instability continued to the present, in that the Gitxsan "have gradually moved into other segments of the cash economy," increasingly do not pursue "an Aboriginal life," and "there is practically no one trapping and hunting full time." Chief Justice McEachern determined that, even in these "Aboriginal pursuits, the plaintiffs do not seem to consider themselves tied to particular territories."[25]

McEachern used the documented record selectively; for instance, although he lauded the use of Hudson's Bay Records, he dismissed the Chief Factor's observations that the Gitxsan actively pursued trapping. According to Gitxsan law, on the contrary, surplus pelts — those that were not used for domestic purposes such as clothing and blankets — were given as gifts at *yukws* and used for gambling,[26] but McEachern concluded that "commercial trapping" was a phenomenon of European contact.[27]

The Chief Justice further concluded that the Royal Proclamation of 1763 had no application or operation in British Columbia, and the "Indian title arising from occupation" had been lawfully extinguished between 1803 and 1858. Subsequent and various Aboriginal rights, after British assertions of sovereignty, existed at the discretion of the Crown. The colonial Crown's intention had been to extinguish First Nations' land rights in order to give unburdened title to newcomers. McEachern felt that fishing was the only "Aboriginal" activity still being exercised and did not require any more territory beyond the existing reserve allocations. For Chief Justice McEachern, Gitxsan "Aboriginality" depended on the practice of fishing, hunting, and gathering throughout the claimed territory; the use of historic territories and activities had been abandoned long ago:

> Witness after witness admitted participation in the wage or cash economy. Art Mathews (*Tenmigyet*), for example, is an enthusiastic weekend aboriginal hunter. Pete Muldoe (*Gitludahl*) has followed a variety of non-aboriginal vocations including logging on the lands claimed by another chief; Joan Ryan (*Hanamuxw*) teaches school in Prince Rupert; and many, many Indians and chiefs have found seasonal or full-time employment in the forest products and coast commercial fishing industry.[28]

Although the Chief Justice had permitted the introduction of oral histories in 1988 as a means of proving ownership,[29] in the end he dismissed most of the oral testimony in which the witnesses themselves could not directly state as fact, or relate, in the case of the Gitxsan, to their *wilp* or house boundaries. What he failed to appreciate was that events and the locations where events occurred were, and are, used by the Gitxsan as maps on the *lax'wiiyip*.

McEachern further contended that what was offered as proof of the *adawaak's* authenticity was personal knowledge and was therefore inherently untrustworthy, in that each *wilp* placed different significance on the private or public use of the *adawaak*. The Chief Justice perceived a serious lack of details about the specific lands the plaintiffs were describing, and noted that the plaintiffs sought to authenticate the *adawaaks* by referencing published material that did not tie the narratives to the *lax'wiiyip* themselves. Furthermore, as McEachern pointed out, many of the published *adawaaks* contained references to historic phenomena such as guns, the Hudson's Bay Company, and peoples outside the statement of claim area, and the *adawaaks* to which the witnesses referred were not exclusive to the Gitxsan people.[30] McEachern, it would appear, placed emphasis on the mythological or legendary characteristics of the accounts instead of their legal meaning — i.e., boundaries, how rights were allocated, how transgressions were adjudicated, how subsistence activities were to be carried out, and, above all, the instruments of authority within the community and how disputes where to be resolved.

The *adawaaks* of the Gitxsan and other West Coast First Nations oral histories and related property before *Delgam'Uukw* (1991) were defined as "myth or legends about their past," and were analyzed in terms of how they contributed to their rich cultural and artistic life.[31] Ethnographers Franz Boas (1899-1915) and Marius Barbeau (1915-1957) recorded narratives, photographed totem poles and other regalia, and generally treated the *adawaaks* and *ayuks* as traditions that were on the verge of disappearing. The period from 1899 through to the 1960s is known as "salvage ethnography," where teams of ethnographers would go into the field and collect the languages, narratives, ceremonies, cultural practices, clothing, and religious artefacts of indigenous cultures that were thought to be on the verge of extinction. Ethnographers focused on the historic social structures, ceremonial life, and cultural uses of images and narratives. Boas recorded hundreds of narratives throughout the Northwest, and his analyses emphasized both the unique material cultures of specific societies as well as where stories and social organizational attributes intersected among the different cultural groups.[32] Boas's work, though immensely important, did not tie the specific *wilp* histories to specific territories or governance practices, and though the Gitxsan are sometimes allied to the Nisga'a and Tsimshian and share many of the narratives analyzed, they are only obliquely alluded to in Boas's work.

Barbeau worked with William Beynon, one of Boas's informants, who held the *wam* of *Gusgai'in* among the Coast Gitlan, but he, too, continued to place significance on the mythological and ceremonial nature of collected narratives, with a similar oblique reference to governance and territory. Unlike Boas, however, Barbeau recorded a wider range of narratives from Gitxsan, Nisga'a, and Coast Tsimshian communities.[33] The comparatively recent work by ethnographer John Cove, who further analyzed the texts collected by Beynon and Barbeau, again gives the impression that the *adawaaks* are stories situated in the Gitxsan past.[34] The point is that one has to understand the cosmology of the Gitxsan, who are associated with general Tsimshian culture, in order to comprehend how authority and influence in the community are held. As anthropologist Marie-François Guedon has said, "There is between the play and reality a very thin line which is easily crossed when one remembers that in the Tsimshian cosmology all representations, all images of an event or entity, call the power of that event back into action."[35]

In terms of reconciliation, Guedon's comment and the other ethnographers' analyses are especially apt, for they show that Gitxsan cultural life has remained constant, despite the assimilative pressures of Canadian life. These records and the interpretations of the *adawaaks*, in conjunction with the testimony of the *Simgigyet* and *Sigidim haanak'a* given at trial between 1987 and 1990, as well as the affidavits and commissioned evidence, illustrate a high degree of fidelity. This corpus of material can be read as an indicator of how much the Gitxsan continue to rely on, and refer to, their *adawaak*. It was further evident during the trial that the purpose of the *adawaak* was to bring the past into the present, to show that the *ayooks* given to the Gitxsan people promote respectful relations, not only among the *wilps*, but also among the Gitxsan and the animals.

With respect to the "proof of the authenticity of the *adawaak*," and lack of detail about the land in the *adawaaks*, Chief Justice McEachern failed to see that it was unimportant that the events coincide directly with the landscape as the province understood it, but how the *Simgigyet* and *Sigidim haanak'a* saw and used the land, how they were able to assert their authority over it, and enlist the co-operation of the members of their *wilp*, their *wil'na t'ahl*, and the *wilksiwitxw* to access resources for their mutual benefit. The Gitxsan, in other words, turned to the remembered knowledge in the *adawaak* of each *wilp* and the associations established through the recounting of the *wilp's adawaak* in conjunction with other *adawaaks* from other *wilps*. The *adawaaks* speak directly to the calamities that were cast onto the Gitxsan for disrespecting the animals, as well as their relations with each other. The *ayooks* were given to all Gitxsan in order that the *huwilp* could co-exist in mutual respect. McEachern recalled in great detail that, although *Sigidim haanak'as Gyolgyet* and *Antigulilbix* knew the history of their *wilps* and spoke comprehensibly about their legends, neither were deeply familiar with the boundaries of territories,[36] which suggested to him that their territories were not "held exclusively." What he missed was that Gitxsan people through their *Simgigyet* and *Sigidim haanak'a* can only control access to the *lax'wiiyip* they claim as their own, subject to its responsibility directly to provide for *wilp*, related *wilp*, and non-*wilp* livelihoods, and any lien of access for another *wilp's* contribution to the funeral costs of one of their members, and for the loss of life at the hands of one of their members. Thus, exclusivity is relative to the affiliations the *wilp* has with other *huwilps*, and its obligations.

"There are far too many inconsistencies in the plaintiffs' evidence to permit me to conclude that individual chiefs or Houses have discrete aboriginal rights or interests in the various territories defined by the internal boundaries," McEachern concluded.[37]

What the Chief Justice did not understand was that the *adawaaks* are told in the context of the governance of the *wilp*, and it is within the telling of, and referencing of, current business that territorial boundaries are maintained, access shared, and disputes settled. Furthermore, *adawaaks*, though exclusive to the *wilp*, are shared with others in the region. This shared exclusivity reinforces bonds based in marriage and kinship, as people from various villages can speak of common origins.[38] It is through public performances — the telling of, or listening to, the *adawaak* at the *yukw* — that property relations within the *wilp*, and to other *wilps*, are declared.[39] The *adawaak* is where the record of the degree of exclusivity of territoriality is maintained among, first, the Gitxsan, and then their neighbours, the Tsimshian, Nisga'a, Gitanyow, Tahltan/Stikine, Tsetsaut, Kaska-Dene, and Carrier-Sekani peoples.[40] It is at the *yukw* that *wilp* property is accounted for, and, more importantly, re-distributed back to the community.[41]

As well as considering and rejecting the claims of ownership of the Gitxsan, Chief Justice McEachern examined and rejected their claims to governance. It is clear that he ignored the opening statement by *Simgigyets Delgam'Uukw* and *Gisday Wa*, where it was said that the purpose of the trial was to "find a place for Gitxsan and Wet'suwet'en law and jurisdiction in Canada."[42] Although they made no argument for sovereignty, the Gitxsan did argue for the inclusion of their law, their jurisdiction, and their social and political institutions. They considered that their claim to ownership entitled them to govern their territory through their own institutions. They claimed the right to ratify land titles, leases, or grants issued by the province after 1984, and that these rights were affirmed by Section 35 of the *Constitution Act, 1982*. They sought provincial-like powers in the areas of land use, social services, health, and education.

Regarding governance, all McEachern could say was that "it was inconceivable that another form of government could exist in the colony after the Crown imposed English law, appointed a Governor with the power to legislate, took title to all the land of the colony and set up the authority of the Crown."[43]

With respect to the post-1871 situation, the Chief Justice continued, "the enactment of the *British North America Act, 1867*, and the adherence to it by the colony of British Columbia in 1871, which was accomplished by Imperial, Canadian and colonial legislation, confirmed the establishment of a federal nation with all legislative powers divided only between Canada and the province."[44]

Conspicuous by its absence is any reference to First Nations' voices as part of the Confederation debates of 1870. There are no records of the responses by Victoria or Ottawa to the petitions sent by the Gitxsan in the 1880s, asking government to meet with them and examine their laws, as a means of integrating them into Canada. In the end, McEachern concluded that "what the Gitksan and Wet'suwet'en witnesses describe as law is really a most uncertain and highly flexible set of customs which are frequently not followed by the Indians themselves."[45]

This further rejection of Gitxsan *ayooks* is particularly strange, as the *Simgigyet* and *Sigidim haanak'a* pay close attention to how access rights to *wilp* resources are allocated and managed. Access is given first to kin and those related through marriage, then through the principles of *amnigwootxw*, or *xkyeehl*. Here the Chief Justice concluded that *amnigwootxw* rights were "so flexible and uncertain that they cannot be classified as laws."[46]

Chief Justice McEachern failed to grasp the essence of Gitxsan property — the right to a livelihood by controlled access to specific territories. Potentially, any one Gitxsan person has access to at least three distinctly different territories; so, in any Gitxsan family, husband and wife, there are at least five areas on which the family can draw. *Amnigwootxw* rights are conferred on a father's children, in order that they may accompany and help him when he goes onto his *wilp's lax'wiiyip* to hunt, fish, gather, or trap. *Amnigwootxw* rights are also given by the *wil'na t'ahl* to the guardians of orphans, in which case a foster family is granted access and other privileges in order that they may raise the orphaned children on their *lax'wiiyip*. *Xkyeehl* rights, like *amnigwootxw* rights, are conferred on a person for a specific period, place, and resource. In essence, the person purchases or leases access to a particular location or resources.

As the legal scholar Mark Walters has suggested, discussion about "Gitxsan lifestyles" may be immaterial, considering that it is the responsibility of the Crown to adhere to the constitutional principle of exclusivity which unmistakably contends that, in order for the Crown to hold title to territory, it must clearly and unequivocally demonstrate that the land discovered was vacant, won in war, or had acquired title purchased in a public forum. Walters advocates, further, that the rights of the First Nations community are bound up in the terms of cession, even if the community has lost its territory through an altercation, and, in situations where the community has yet to cede its territory, the "property rights" associated with their laws remain intact.[47] Neither of these situations occurred before the trial in 1984.

The British Columbia Court of Appeal Decision, 1993[48]

To Gitxsan and Wet'suwet'en people, 8 March 1991 is known as "Black Friday." It was the day the Chief Justice of the British Columbia Supreme Court handed down the *Delgam'Uukw* judgement. The decision, as Chief Joseph Mathias of Squamish noted, had "eliminated the basis to negotiate," suggesting that there "was nothing to compel the parties to come to the table."[49] Though both provincial and federal ministers responsible for Indian Affairs were quick to counter the claim and affirm their commitment to negotiations, the *Delgam'Uukw* decision raised the possibility that land would not be on the table. Jack Weisgerber, the Reform Party Aboriginal Critic, said, "We were brought very quickly to a realization that foremost in the minds of the people we were meeting with was the Land Question," and, "We're going to have to reconsider the context of negotiations."[50]

After the 1991 trial, the provincial position on Aboriginal title changed. The province accepted that First Nations in British Columbia had, at the least, a "political" claim to title, and was willing to negotiate treaties with First Nations. In support of this change in perspective, the Province of British Columbia, Canada, and the First Nations Summit accepted the British Columbia Claims Task Force's Report that provided the mandate for the British Columbia Treaty Commission. In 1993, the British Columbia Treaty Commission Office opened its doors with a mandate to facilitate tripartite agreements that would give First Nations, the federal and provincial Crowns "certainty and finality."[51] Certainty refers to the assurance to Canadians and industry that there are no vagaries with respect to the First Nation's Aboriginal rights or practice, as well as a defined land base and access to specific resources.[52] Although the province conceded for the appeal that there had been no "blanket extinguishment prior to Confederation," and it submitted that some Aboriginal rights may have been extinguished or impaired as a result of the province exercising its right to land and resources under Section 109 of the *Constitution Act, 1867,* the province maintained that the plaintiffs did not have a right of ownership of, or a proprietary interest in, the lands and resources they claimed. The province agreed with the Chief Justice that the plaintiffs had failed to prove they held the claimed lands exclusively. Nor had they proved that they maintained external or internal boundaries. With respect to jurisdiction or self-government, the province also agreed that, though the plaintiffs had lived in organized societies and certain rights or freedoms to self-government may continue to exist, they were subject to the laws of Canada and the province. The province also agreed with the Chief Justice with respect to the weight that was given to the expert evidence and the Hudson's Bay Company records, and supported McEachern's conclusion as to the value of the oral histories. The province agreed, further, that the Chief Justice was correct in characterizing the plaintiffs' Aboriginal rights as *sui generis*, but qualified the point by suggesting that the location, scope, content, and consequence of the plaintiffs' Aboriginal rights remain the subject of negotiation and further judicial consideration.

Although the province had recognized that there was, at least, the "political legitimacy of Aboriginal rights and title and inherent rights to self-government,"[53] the Gitxsan were quick to file an appeal. They felt that negotiating under the assumption that their land and rights had been legally extinguished at the time of "sovereignty" only to be politically resurrected in the *Constitution Act, 1982,* and endorsed by the province, was too ambiguous to achieve the "certainty and finality" they desired. The Gitxsan preferred a position that acknowledged unequivocally their claim to their *lax'wiiyip* and their Aboriginal rights to self-government.

The Majority Decision

The Court of Appeal judgement was handed down on 25 June 1993. All five judges agreed that Aboriginal rights to title existed, based on the modified stance of the province, but they rejected by a margin of three to two contemporary claims of ownership by the Gitxsan.[54] The court clearly incorporated the change in the province's position, in that there was "no blanket extinguishment of title prior to 1871," and the Gitxsan had an existing Aboriginal right of "occupancy and use" over much of the territory claimed. The judges agreed that the extent and content of such title should be left to negotiations.

The majority judgements of Macfarlane (Taggart concurring) and Wallace concluded that the trial judge had made no palpable error in his assessment of the evidence, and they agreed with Chief Justice McEachern's conclusions that any Aboriginal right held by the Gitxsan to exercise jurisdiction over the territory had been extinguished by 1870. The Appeal Court allowed for the possibility that Aboriginal title had not been entirely extinguished by the colony of British Columbia prior to 1871, but, after Confederation, First Nations held non-exclusive Aboriginal title. As Justice Macfarlane stated,

> I do not think that all aboriginal interests in respect of land were extinguished before 1871. They [aboriginal rights or title] could not be extinguished by the Province after 1871. The trial judge held that legislation enacted between 1858 and 1871 providing for the settlement of the colony was completely inconsistent with the continued exercise of aboriginal rights, and that a clear and plain intention to extinguish aboriginal rights should be inferred from that legislation. I am not persuaded aboriginal rights could not coexist with settlement, nor that the Crown intended, by virtue of those legislative steps, to completely negate the Indian interest. Indeed, the British continued to recognize the Indian interest. The Crown promised to preserve and protect Indian settlements. The *Terms of Union, 1871,* between British Columbia and Canada provided that lands would be set aside, and would be transferred to the Dominion for the use and benefit of the Indians, a process not completed until 1938. The courts have continued to give effect to claims in respect of aboriginal rights. For instance, they have recognized unextinguished fishing and hunting rights in places other than reserves, but having a connection with aboriginal lands. All of this supports the conclusion that the pre-Confederation legislation was not clearly and plainly intended to extinguish aboriginal rights.[55]

Speaking about Aboriginal rights, Macfarlane concluded:

> The essential nature of an aboriginal right stems from occupation and use. The right attaches to land occupied and used by aboriginal peoples as their traditional home prior to the assertion of sovereignty. Rights of occupancy are usually exclusive. Other rights, like hunting or fishing, may be shared. What is an aboriginal use may vary from case to case. Aboriginal rights are fact and site specific. They are rights which are integral to the distinctive culture of an aboriginal society. The nature and content of the right, and the area within which the right was exercised, are questions of fact.
>
> The precise bundle of rights that a particular aboriginal community can assert may depend upon a number of factors including the nature, kind and purpose of the use of occupancy of the land by the aboriginal community in question, and the extent to which such use and/or occupancy was exclusive or non-exclusive.[56]

Concerning the claim to governance of the territories in question, Macfarlane agreed with the trial judge that the division of powers at Confederation had extinguished any Gitxsan rights:

> I have said there is no question the Gitksan and Wet'suwet'en people had an organized society. It is pointless to argue that such a society was without traditions, rules and regulations. Insofar as those continue to exist there is no reason why those traditions may not continue so long as members of the Indian community agree to adhere to them. But those traditions, rules and regulations cannot operate if they are in conflict with laws of the Province or of Canada. In 1871, when British Columbia joined Confederation, legislative power was divided between Canada and the provinces. The division exhausted the source of such power. Any form of Indian self-government, then existing, was superseded by the *Constitution Act, 1867*, as adopted by the Province in 1871.[57]

As legal scholar Robert Freedman has pointed out, there was a degree of ambiguity surrounding the meaning of self-government, and this may have had its basis in how the pleadings themselves were set out. In the statement of claim, the Gitxsan asked the courts to "recognize that they governed themselves" according to their own laws, and that they have the right to govern themselves. Such a statement, Freedman suggests, could entail anything from a measure of self-regulation in their home territories to the ability to enact laws, independent of Canada or British Columbia, through their own institutions. Matters of what privileges an Indigenous community retains or modifies with respect to governance is an exercise that is best suited for nego-tiations.[58] When speaking about jurisdiction, however, Macfarlane supported the trial judge and elaborated on his conclusion:

> Rights to self-government, encompassing a power to make general laws governing the land and resources in the territory, and the people in that territory, can only be described as legislative powers. They serve to limit provincial legislative jurisdiction in the territory and to allow the plaintiffs to establish a third order of government in Canada. Putting the proposition in another way: the jurisdiction of the plaintiffs would diminish the provincial and federal share of the total distribution of legislative power in Canada.[59]

"Furthermore," Macfarlane concluded, "the claim to the right to control and manage the use of the lands and resources in the territories cannot succeed because the plaintiffs failed to establish the necessary ownership needed to support such a jurisdiction."[60]

Responding to the plaintiffs' pleadings that they continued to hold juris-diction, Justice Wallace stated:

> Jurisdiction or self-government includes the power to pass laws which will be recognized by the community in question, and the ability to en-force such laws. Prior to the acquisition of sovereignty over British Co-lumbia, the Indians exercised jurisdiction in the territory to the extent made possible by their social organization. However, once sovereignty was asserted, the Indians became subjects of the Crown and the com-mon law applied throughout the territory and to all inhabitants.[61]

Wallace determined that:

> After the exercise of sovereignty by the Crown, the plaintiffs no longer retained the aboriginal right of self-government or jurisdiction over any part of the territory or the members of their House. Any rights of self-regulation must arise from agreement between the plaintiffs and

the provincial or federal Crown or by decision of the trial court. The plaintiffs established a non-exclusive aboriginal right of traditional occupancy and use of that portion of territory designated by the trial judge.[62]

It is surprising that the analysis of self-regulation or self-government was interpreted in such narrow and absolute terms. The British constitutional principle of continuity would seem to imply that First Nations have a right to govern themselves according to their law in all matters, except where Aboriginal law and the common law would intersect. In such situations — natural justice concerns, for example, or when the Crown's sovereignty is placed in jeopardy — it is expected that both parties be afforded the respect of sitting in council to come to agreement as to the shape of the law, as well as the remedy. Outside these concerns, First Nations have the right both to govern themselves and to expect protection from third-party interest, as well as the co-operation of the Crown in safeguarding rights. Such a proposition shifts the discussion away from site-specific land or resource-based rights, situated in historical practices, to one that may see the integration of the management of the land of territories in question alongside provincial ministries.

The Minority Decision

Justice Lambert, drawing on the "settlement rule"[63] and the Doctrine of Continuity,[64] which states that the local law in newly acquired territories continues at common law, said that Aboriginal title was only one aspect of Aboriginal rights, and, as a right, it had its origins in the First Nations societies that existed before European settlers arrived. Lambert contended that, at the time of contact and declaration of sovereignty, these rights continued, and warranted recognition and protection under the common law.[65]

"If, either before or after the beginning of the process of settlement, Sovereignty was asserted by the Crown," Lambert maintained, "that Sovereignty would carry with it the power to make just laws for all the inhabitants of the land over which Sovereignty was asserted, but Sovereignty itself would not displace the existing rights and social system of the indigenous people."[66]

According to Lambert, it follows that, when the Crown asserted sovereignty and adopted the common law as the law over the territories in question, then it would be the common law itself that recognized, adopted, and affirmed the rights and titles of the Indigenous peoples. Unless the laws of the

Indigenous peoples were inconsistent with sovereignty itself, or inconsistent with the laws made applicable to the whole territory and with the principles of fundamental justice, the common law would have adopted the laws of the Indigenous peoples as well. Arguably, then, the desire of the Gitxsan to integrate their laws and governance procedures in a limited area, may not be contrary to the goals of the Crown and could be achieved by modifying the fundamental relationship the Crown has established with the community in question — i.e., one that is co-operative with Aboriginal rights, and would include a degree of independence with respect to self-government.

Lambert's explanation of the nature of Aboriginal rights may have provided the basis for analyzing the content of those rights not as specific activities but the *sui generis* nature and intent of the title rights. "Accordingly," he stated, "I think that a different approach is required, an approach that tries to characterize aboriginal rights in terms of aboriginal society rather than western society."[67]

Following *Sparrow*,[68] Lambert suggested that the analysis of the right in question "must uphold the honour of the Crown," and "must be in keeping with the unique contemporary relationship, grounded in history and policy, between the Crown and Canada's aboriginal peoples." Thus, Aboriginal rights that warrant protection may in fact be the "integral and distinctiveness"[69] qualities that tie the community to particular locations, relationships among themselves, beliefs about who they are, and how they must act toward the land and each other. Thus, according to Lambert, the purpose of Section 35 was not to protect First Nations rights as they were in 1778:

> Its purpose must have been to secure to Indian people, without further erosion, a modern unfolding of the rights flowing from the fact that, before settlers with their new Sovereignty arrived, the Indians occupied the land, possessed its resources, and used and enjoyed both the land and resources through a social system which they controlled through their own institutions. That modern unfolding must come not only in legal rights, but, more importantly, in the reflection of those rights in a social organization and in an economic structure which will permit the Indian peoples to manage their affairs with both some independence from the remainder of Canadian society and also with honourable interdependence between all parts of the Canadian social fabric.[70]

This type of relationship requires that the Crown examine Gitxsan laws and legal institutions, especially the community's relationship to its land and political organization:

> They are not asserting a claim to govern themselves within the geographical boundaries of the territory. They are claiming the right to manage and control the exercise of the community right of possession, occupation, use and enjoyment of the land and its resources which constitutes their aboriginal title, and they are claiming the right to organize their social system on those matters that are an integral part of their distinctive culture in accordance with their own customs, traditions, and practices, which define their culture.[71]

The rights of use and enjoyment of their Aboriginal title lands and the ability to participate in the management of their affairs is situated in the Doctrine of Continuity, according to which the laws of the Aboriginal community, unless they are extinguished or modified through negotiation, remain intact:

> The Gitksan and Wet'suwet'en people had rights of self-government and self-regulation in 1846, at the time of sovereignty. Those rights rested on customs, traditions and practices of those people to the extent that they formed an integral part of their distinctive cultures. The assertion of British Sovereignty only took away rights that were inconsistent with the concept of British Sovereignty. The introduction of British Law into British Columbia was only an introduction of such laws as were not from local circumstances inapplicable. The existence of a body of Gitksan and Wet'suwet'en customary law would be expected to render much of the newly introduced English law inapplicable to the Gitksan and Wet'suwet'en people, particularly since none of the institutions of English law were available to them in their territory, so their local circumstances would tend to have required the continuation of their own laws. The division of powers brought about when British Columbia entered into confederation in 1871 would not, in my opinion, have made any difference to Gitksan and Wet'suwet'en customary laws. Since 1871, Provincial laws of general application would apply to the Gitksan and Wet'suwet'en people, and Federal laws, particularly the *Indian Act*, would apply to them. But to the extent that Gitksan and Wet'suwet'en customary law lay at the core

of their Indianness, that law would not be abrogated by Provincial law of general application nor by Federal law, unless those Federal laws demonstrated a clear and plain intention of the Sovereign power in parliament to abrogate the Gitksan and Wet'suwet'en customary laws. Subject to those overriding considerations, Gitksan and Wet'suwet'en customary laws of self-government and self-regulation have continued to the present day and are now constitutionally protected by s. 35 of the *Constitution Act, 1982.*[72]

The Gitxsan in the past put aside many sanctions that the *Lixs giigyet* found too harsh. Likewise, they modified their *Li'ligit* in order that the *Lixs giigyet* were not offended by the practice of it, and placed limits on their ritual obligations to each other. After the fire in 1872, they accepted that they would speak within the law. In 1888, they further agreed to defer to the "white man's law" to settle disputes. In 1993 they argued in the Court of Appeal that they had laid out their land tenure system and governing institutions, and these reflected the essential characteristics of ownership. It was thus within their distinctive land tenure system that self-government was described. The Gitxsan claim that they have not relinquished their right to harvest resources in their territories.

Although the majority decision in the 1993 Court of Appeal case supported the trial decision with respect to title and self-government, the minority decision raised enough ambiguity as to the soundness of title in British Columbia to warrant the Gitxsan entering into treaty talks. The dissenting opinions acknowledged that Gitxsan rights to their territory were communal in nature, and that a declaration of sovereignty by the Crown did not necessarily abrogate their rights to self-regulation for the preservation and enhancement of their own social, political, cultural, linguistic, and spiritual identity. They concluded that land use outside of, as well as adjacent to, Gitxsan villages could be determined either by another trial or by agreement.[73]

The Negotiation Interlude

The *Simgigyet* and *Sigidim haanak'a* in 1884 were clear that, as owners, they were willing to sit down and discuss how, by whom, and for what purpose the land was to be used. The *Simgigyet* of Gitwangak petitioned Victoria to stop miners from staking claims up the Lorne Creek without their permission. In 1889, *Simgigyet Gyetm Galdoo* from Gitanmaax appealed again to the government to stop the *Lixs giigyet* from occupying the land without Gitxsan permission. In 1908 and 1909, the Gitxsan again tried, through petitions and hearings, to address the title question. In 1915, at the McKenna-McBride hearings, each *Simgigyet* presented an argument concerning the unresolved Land Question, only to be told that the commission's mandate was limited to the size of reserve lands, and had no authority over the title question. When the federal cabinet modified its position to negotiate comprehensive claims after the *Calder* decision in 1973, the Gitxsan were once again prepared to negotiate. In October 1984, they filed their statement of claim, intending to challenge the province's position regarding Aboriginal title and rights, with the aim of aligning their traditional governance and territorial holdings with that of the provincial and federal Crowns.

Prior to the Court of Appeal hearing in 1991, the Gitxsan elected not to accept British Columbia's offer to enter treaty negotiations until there was a clearer position on Aboriginal title. While the majority decision of the Court of Appeal endorsed many of Chief Justice McEachern's findings, they did overrule him on the issue of pre-Confederation blanket extinguishment of Aboriginal title, and they spoke to the urgency of a negotiated settlement.

Although the Gitxsan did not achieve as decisive a ruling as they desired, and while the negative findings on the nature of Aboriginal title and the rejection of their claim to self-government argued strongly in favour of taking an appeal to the Supreme Court of Canada, the Gitxsan nevertheless were resolved to give negotiations a chance, and entered into an agreement with British Columbia and Canada. The intent of the Accord of Respect and Recognition was "to seek an adjournment, for a period of one year, from the Supreme Court of Canada, of the appeal in *Delgam'Uukw* v. *British Columbia* in order for all three parties to negotiate a settlement." The Accord stipulated that the tri-partite process should be able to reach a treaty within 18 months, with the option of a further continuance on the adjournment of the appeal to the Supreme Court of Canada, if negotiations were going well.[74]

For the Gitxsan, certainty could be achieved in the Statement of Intent area through agreements with Canada that outlined the Gitxsan commitment to Canada. The Gitxsan also wanted a commitment from Canada that would see the current level of funding maintained for language, culture, health, and community infrastructure. It was assumed that the Gitxsan would take control of existing reserve lands, capital and revenue trusts, and would be able to base their self-government on the *wilp* system. In the Statement of

Intent Area, the Gitxsan contended that the optimum relationship with the provincial government was based on the co-management of resources and services with the appropriate provincial ministry.[75] Thus, the Gitxsan vision of "finality" was a working relationship among *huwilp* and provincial ministries. The Gitxsan looked to write a series of agreements with provincial ministries (especially forestry) that incorporated access to actual and potential resources throughout their *lax'wiiyip* either through employment guarantees or by revenue sharing. The over-riding aim was to channel revenue from resource extraction back into the region to support self-government.

Gitxsan, provincial, and federal negotiations lasted for five months. The province suspended negotiations on 1 February 1996, citing fundamental differences "on the nature and scope of aboriginal rights and jurisdiction."[76] The province also elected not to renew the Accord, having determined that many of the broader issues between British Columbia and the Gitxsan would "first require the Supreme Court of Canada to decide the *Delgam'Uukw* appeal."[77]

The Federal Deputy Minister, Scott Serson, held a different view:

Slow but steady progress has been made at the treaty table with the Gitxsan. There are clearly different points of view in a number of areas, but this is understandable and expected at this early stage of the negotiations. British Columbia has indicated their willingness to continue to negotiate these matters with the Wet'suwet'en. In our view there is every reason to continue to negotiate the same matters at the treaty table with the Gitxsan.[78]

These words did not move the province to reconsider its stance. The Gitxsan felt that the province was unwilling to contemplate any perspective that deviated from its interpretation of the Court of Appeal's majority decision in *Delgam'Uukw,* which, although it acknowledged that there had been "no blanket extinguishment of title prior to 1871," limited the right to site-specific activities in which the extent and content were to be left to negotiations.

The province's position was that any self-government rights were limited to reserve lands, and site- and activity-specific rights. Similarly, any self-government parameters were limited to existing *Indian Act* management arrangements.[79] Although all parties had been encouraged to negotiate a settlement, it became impossible to continue. As John Cashore, the provincial Minister responsible for Aboriginal Affairs, said, "We are simply not making any progress." The Gitxsan chief negotiator was more candid. "Politically," Don Ryan contended, the government was "afraid to make any decisions."[80]

Delgam'Uukw v. *British Columbia*, 1997[81]

The Supreme Court of Canada deviated from the traditional attitude that denied title to First Nations communities who had not first entered into agreements of surrender. It stated clearly that "title existed, until it was lawfully extinguished," and, as the trial court had ignored the oral histories and other testimony of the Gitxsan and Wet'suwet'en people, which in the Supreme Court of Canada's eyes would have enabled the lower courts to conclude that the Gitxsan and Wet'suwet'en held Aboriginal title in their territories, granted the Gitxsan a retrial. The court elaborated on the content of Aboriginal title as that encompassing an area larger than existing reserves and broader than site-specific activities which have been defined by Aboriginal rights activities. Thus, Aboriginal title confers upon the holders a broader range of rights that could include forestry, mining, and oil and gas development. As a means of reconciling the past occupation of the First Nations community with that of the Crown, the Supreme Court ruled that Aboriginal title rights could compete with other property rights: the community had the right of consultation, and could press for compensation. The community right of consultation, in the eyes of the court, was more than mere notice: the community had the right of refusal, especially where their hunting, trapping, gathering, or fishing rights would be severely affected. As part of this reconciliation, the Court specified that compensation was due, and like the BC Court of Appeal, encouraged the parties to negotiate rather than litigate.

The court postponed the issue of self-government to another day.

For the Gitxsan, the Supreme Court decision meant two things. First, they could continue to use their *ayooks* as the basis for negotiation, including their boundaries. Second, they could put forward their social and political structure as justifications for continuing to hold onto ownership; they could establish federal protection for their Aboriginal rights and title in their *lax'wiiyip* as well as establish a basis for an ongoing working relationship with British Columbia in the area of resource management.

In terms of reconciliation, the Gitxsan have the opportunity to take their title concerns back to court. The Supreme Court of Canada has, in its definition of Aboriginal title, laid the foundation for negotiations to proceed. A First Nations community which has not surrendered its title to the Crown is not required to surrender it as a precursor to most economic endeavours, except where the use of the territory conflicts with the nature of the community's "Indianness." For the Gitxsan, their Indianness is bound up in the social and political institutions that require them to respect the animals, the *lax'wiiyip,* and each other. Also, the Supreme Court of Canada, even though it has enlarged the scope of infringement onto Aboriginal title to include most legislative initiatives, requires that the Crown engage in meaningful consultation, and accommodate First Nations rights.

CHAPTER FOUR

Gitxsan Property, Ownership, and Governance

GITXSAN SOCIETY RESTS ON THE FOUNDATION OF THE WILP. WILP MEMBERSHIP may include anywhere from 25 to upwards of 200 people at any given time. Currently, there are about ten thousand Gitxsan people, and approximately 80 per cent of them live in or around their historic villages in north-central British Columbia. The *wilp* is the basic social and political unit in Gitxsan society. The term *wilp* means, literally, the dwelling place of a family, and it is the resource-owning group. *Wilp* membership is restricted to the *Sigidim haanak'a* or *Simgigyet*, her or his brothers, sisters, sisters' children, and sisters' daughters' children.

Collectively, the *wilp* owns its history, the *adawaaks,* which are associated with the *wilp's* symbols of title (*ayuks*) to its territory (*lax'wiiyip*). *Ayuks* are displayed on various ceremonial regalia — *gwiis gan 'malaa* (robes or blankets), *'am halitx* (headdresses), and *am bilan* (aprons) — and *t'saan* (poles) at different *li'ligit* (feasts). There are 64 *wilps* associated with the Gitxsan *lax'wiiyip*. Gitxsan society, like that of other Northwest Coast peoples, is divided into four groups called *pteex*. The *pteex* existed before the deluge, when all lived at *T'am Lax amit*. When the people scattered after the deluge, they carried with them their *pteex* affiliation. *Pteex* membership is inherited through the mother, and marriage partners are sought outside it. To marry inside that *pteex* is to commit incest. One is born into, socialized by, and inherits from one's mother's family.

According to Gitxsan historian Susan Marsden,[1] after the people dug themselves out from under the snows, the people of the *Genada-Laxsel pteex* (the Frog/Raven Clan) were the first to return to the *lax'wiiyip*, the great plateau to the northwest. The *Laxgibuu* (the Wolf Clan) followed, then the

Laxskiik (the Eagle Clan), and finally the *Gisk'aast pteexs* (the Fireweed Clan). After the dispersal, some members of the *Genada-Laxsel pteex* stayed on Haida Gwaii (the Queen Charlotte Islands) while others travelled to Alaska. The *Laxgibuu* lived on the north coast for a while but were forced back up the Nass River by the Tlingit, and lastly some *Laxskiik* from the Nass River region moved down into Upper Skeena and finally to Kitwanga (Gitwankga). The *Gisk'aast pteexs* moved in from the north. The return to the *lax'wiiyip* occurred *wilp* by *wilp*, and, according to the *adawaak*, those of common *pteex* assisted each other and settled in paired *pteex* groups at village sites along the banks of major rivers near canyons or by productive fishing sites.

Pteex affiliation, like the inheritance of *wilp* property rights and political status, is determined by matrilineal inheritance. Those who are of the same *pteex* consider themselves to have been at one time related or from the same village before the flood and are thought of as family; they refer to each other as *wil'na t'ahl* (true or fictive first cousins). The *wil'na t'ahl* are called on to assist with the funeral when one of the *wilp* members passes on; they are called as support workers for the necessary *li'ligit* that affirms the succession of a *Simgigyet* and *Sigidim haanak'a*, and in situations where additional help or labour is required by any of the affiliated *wilps*.

In historic times, each family had a dwelling in its village of origin, and although male *wilp* members usually did not leave this village, in most cases women moved to their husband's uncle's village when they married. The woman's sons or daughters at puberty would return to their mother's village to be trained by their mother's brother to become either the *Simgigyet* or the *Sigidim haanak'a*. While either a man or a woman can hold the title, the preferred head of the *wilp* is one's mother's uncle, brother, or nephew. Early training in the *ayooks* (laws) and history of the Gitxsan is the responsibility of one's father's *wilp* (the *wilksiwitxw*). This body maintains special relationships with the child they have educated throughout his or her life. The *wilksiwitxw* provides the first and last bed of any child, and assists with the ceremonial obligations of these children, from sponsoring one's naming *li'ligits* to paying for special events at one's funeral. More importantly, while one's father is alive, one has access to particular fishing sites, hunting grounds, or berry grounds, as well as trapping privileges in one's father *wilp's lax'wiiyip*. Thus, one's *wilksiwithxw* assists the *wilp* in establishing the next generation, and knits the society together.

Besides these lateral alliances that cement Gitxsan society and affiliation with other *wilps* through the *wilksiwitxw* (or *wilksiwitxw* members who reside in other villages), the Gitxsan *wilp* becomes the pivot around which relationships with other communities occur. Although the property of the *wilp* is maintained through adherence to a matrilineal inheritance system, social and economic relations throughout the region are maintained through marriage, knowing the *wilp's* place of origin as remembered in the *adawaak*, and by acknowledging the importance of *pteex* affiliation. Political and social aggregation among the Gitxsan rests on the foundation established by *wilp* membership, and is interwoven with claims of exclusivity to specific territories, various titles, and histories by the *wilp* that are tempered by the desire to maintain access to additional territories and economic endeavours.

The *wilp* is the property-holding group, and its members have rights and obligations. Only members of the *wilp*, directed by the *Simgigyet* and *Sigidim haanak'a*, may transact business associated with the *wilp's lax'wiiyip*, *ayuks*, or *wams* (names). Although Gitxsan villages in themselves do not form political and social units, *wilp* members who live in the villages are usually more or less central, or at least close to the *wilp's lax'wiiyip*. In times of crisis, villages will align themselves against a common enemy, or, as in contemporary times, unite under the banner of the Gitxsan Hereditary Chief Society (or the Gitxsan Treaty Society) to put forward their legal actions and now their treaty negotiations. The relationship is best described as an alliance of *wilps*, or *Gim litxwid*.

As part of the Gitxsan's renewed contract with the animals after the deluge, they were to remember the events that banished them from the *lax'wiiyip*, and the *Sigidim haanak'as* were entrusted to manage the resources in the *wilp lax'wiiyip*, as well as maintain respectful relations between the *huwilp* and *wilp* members. Besides the respect that they were to show to each other and their *wil'na t'ahl* (related *wilps* of the same *pteex*), they were to acknowledge the contributions of their *wilksiwitxw* (the father's relatives). This is remembered in the *adawaaks*. Thus, the purpose of the *adawaak* is to bring the past into the present, and to show that the *Ayooks* of *Naa hlimoot'* (laws of sharing) given to the Gitxsan promote respectful relations.[2]

Respectful relations must exist not only among the *huwilp*, but also between the Gitxsan and the animals. Historically, First Nations' traditional political and legal life is considered to have been replaced by the *Indian Act* and compliance with federal and provincial laws. The Gitxsan can illustrate, however, that several groups or individuals may hold different kinds of rights in the same resource or land. It could be said that individual rights in resources or land, as Gordon Wilson contends, are dependent on social relationships, and even then the individual can only have definite rights to participate in the use of or share the produce from particular locations, governed by specific rules.[3] Rights to resources for members of a community, as Max Gluckman has suggested, are determined by status inside it, and by meeting obligations inherent in that status.[4] Thus, the Gitxsan *Simgigyet* and *Sigidim haanak'a* must carry the responsibility of managing their *lax'wiiyip* in such a manner that will enable the *wilp* members to have enough to eat. Similarly, *wilp* members and those affiliated with the *wilp*, regardless of political status, must respect the *ayooks* and heed the word of the *Simgigyet* and *Sigidim haanak'a*.

At the same time, Gitxsan society, like most societies, is organized and governed according to principles that first maintain that the *lax'wiiyip*, the traditional territory of the *wilps,* is owned as a whole in alliance with each other, and then individual *wilp* members are delegated rights according to relationships and in particular territories, suggesting that all land can be considered communal in nature, whether it is land in nation states or in stateless societies. By relying on terms such as "communal," "ownership," "beneficial occupation," or "usufruct," however, one might be masking the real pattern of rights to land and/or resources, as Robert Lowie has argued.[5] Fundamentally, the Gitxsan are corporate group owners of the *lax'wiiyip* that is associated with a specific *Simgigyet* or *Sigidim haanak'a*. The *Simgigyet* or *Sigidim haanak'a* have the authority, in the name of the *wilp*, to assign to others, family and non-family alike, the right to procure food resources throughout the *lax'wiiyip*. They are also responsible for managing the resources, and must account to the *wilp* for their decisions.

Wilp Property and Ownership

For the Gitxsan, the *lax'wiiyip* is part of them, their status, and their history. On 12 May 1987, *Delgam'Uukw* and *Gisday Wa*[6] stated in their opening address to the court:

> For us, the ownership of the territory is a marriage of the chief and the land. Each chief has an ancestor who encountered and acknowledged the life of the land. From such encounters comes power. The land, the plants, the animals and the people, all have spirit; they all must be shown respect. That is the basis of our law.
>
> The Chief is responsible for ensuring that all the people in his house respect the land, and all living things. When a Chief directs his House

properly and the laws are followed, then that original power can be recreated. That is the source of the Chief's authority.

My power is carried in my House's histories, songs, dances and the crests. It is recreated at the feast when the histories are told, the songs and the dances performed and the crests displayed. With the wealth that comes from respectful use of the territory, the House feeds the name of the chief in the feast hall. In this way, the law, the Chief, the territory and feast become one. The unity of the Chief's authority and his House's ownership of its territory are witnessed and thus affirmed by other chiefs at the feast.

By following the law, the power flows from the land to the people through the Chief; by using the wealth of the territory, the House feasts its Chief so he can properly fulfil the law.[7]

Delgam'Uukw and *Gisday Wa* claimed that, as they held the name of a *Simgigyet*, they held title, and the property of the *wilp* was part of the status named by that title. As *Simgigyets,* they are responsible for ensuring that the people of their *wilp* have enough to eat and respect the land and all living things in and on it. When the *Simgigyet* directs *wilp* members properly, and the laws are followed, the power of the *wilp* is recreated. It is in the name of the *wilp* that the *Simgigyet* has the authority to direct its members on *wilp lax'wiiyip*.

Holding the title of *Simgigyet* also asserted a justification for Canada and British Columbia to negotiate with *Delgam'Uukw* and *Gisday Wa* as property owners, and to view their title in terms of their laws and obligations. The Gitxsan desire to have both proprietary and management interests in the salmon fishery, in their trap lines, in the berries they gather, and the animals they hunt recognized. They want to be able to exert an appropriate influence over federal and provincial policy decisions with respect to resource allocation, permitting Gitxsan law to affect these interests throughout the *lax'wiiyip*. In the event of an infringement as a result of Crown appropriation or third party damage, trespass, or nuisance, they believe it is necessary that they be involved to set the conditions for appropriation and in the determination of standards for compensation.

For the Gitxsan, tenure and ownership lie coded in a series of cultural images and practices, and in their historic relationship to the land. Similarly, Gitxsan leadership, though hereditary, is contingent on responsible behaviour and the fulfilling of duties and obligations. Access to resources is granted first to immediate family members, and second to spouses of family members and their children. Generally, Gitxsan property, like common law property, has to do with the rights of persons to access resources for food, ceremony, and economic pursuits. Gitxsan *wilp* property is firmly situated in the fact that persons do not necessarily have rights over things, but owe obligations to one another. Thus, Gitxsan property laws consist of principles that sustain particular practices, such as fishing, hunting, and sharing, the authority to organize labour and to have access to food. This authority starts with listening to the *adawaak*, acknowledging the *ayuks,* and finally, abstracting the principles of law that become embedded in events such as fishing, hunting, gathering, and sharing.

Since Gitxsan status is tied to governance roles, which are situated in specific locations with particular duties, the *lax'wiiyip* and the wealth that is held on it is an intricate and vital component of Gitxsan public and private life. The *nax nox,* or power, that the *wilp* holds is contingent on respectful use of the territory, which, in turn, is reflected in the well-being of all members. These features stem from the capacity of the *wilp* to hold exclusivity over their *lax'wiiyip* against other w*ilps*. This right of exclusivity is further coupled with a correlative duty of other w*ilps* to agree to stay out of the territories in question, unless permission is given. The *Sigidim haanak'a*, in addition, has the obligation to maintain the ecological integrity of the *lax'wiiyip* in order that the fish, birds, animals, and plants will continue to exist, and that all *wilp* members have plenty to eat. They are stewards of the land, rivers, and air. For it is on the land that, individually and collectively, the Gitxsan encounter life, and it is when the narratives and songs are told and performed at the feasts that the authority of the *Sigidim haanak'a* is legitimized. The display of crests, the narratives, and the bounty fed to guests lays the foundation for the subsequent affirmation or refutation of property decisions by the management of the *wilp*.

Adawaaks

The *wilp* first owns its history, the *adawaaks*, which, as charter narratives, outline the migrations back into the *lax'wiiyip*, the relationships among *pteex* relatives, and the *lax'wiiyip* boundaries. In some cases, the *adawaaks* relate inter-*wilp* tensions and inter-community wars. They record *wilp* origins, migrations and the territory of each *wilp*. Also encoded in the *adawaaks* are the individual symbols of title, the crests or *ayuks* that give the *wilp* the right to occupy and use the territory it claims. *Adawaaks*, as *Gyologyet* explained at trial, are central to Gitxsan life and are considered the primary aspect of *wilp* property and knowledge:

> *Adawaak* in the Gitksan language is a powerful word for describing what the House stands for, what the territory stands for, is the *adawaak*. It's not a story, it's how the people travelled back into the territory. This is the *adawaak*. And it's the most important thing in Gitksan, is to have an *adawaak*. Without an *adawaak* you can't very well say you are a chief or you own a territory. Without the *adawaak* — it has to come first, the *adawaak* — names come after, songs come after, crests come after it, and the territory that's held, fishing places — all those come into one, and that's the *adawaak*.[8]

The *adawaak* is history, she said, and they tell "how the Gitxsan people have their names right from infant to a chief. The *adawaak* refers to the songs that are made for the purpose of each chief to use. The *adawaak* tells of the *nax nox*, why it was created and how it's shown amongst the people in the Feast House. The *adawaak* also tells of the territory of the chief." [9]

Ayuks

The *ayuks* are sets of symbols that bind the *wilp* to their *lax'wiiyip* and to the animals from the time before the floods. The symbols illustrate to others the *wilp's* territorial holdings and their relationship to other *wilps*. These symbols, the *ayuks*, as *Xamlaxyeltxw* testified, "are always acquired from the territory, and in the ancient time it was very hard to get these *ayuks*. . . . Each house has its own *ayuks*, and no-one from another house is supposed to use another house's *ayuk*, or crest.[10] According to *Ax Gwin Desxw*, these *ayuks* are "very important symbols to Gitksan people":

> The *ayuk* shows how the house groups attained their land initially, who inhabits a particular piece of land, or how they killed different animals. The *ayuk* clearly identifies who you are, and to which house group you belong. *Ayuks* define how much land you have, how much power you have, and your authority over that piece of land. Nobody just goes up and uses somebody's *ayuks*, because if you try and take somebody's *ayuks* you are taking their land away.

For instance, people like *Tenmigyet* in Gitwankga, their *ayuks* are the bear cubs. Our house has the grizzly bear with the two baby bear cubs on the ears. This identifies who I am, and I know who *Tenmigyet* is because I know what his *ayuks* are. And those *ayuks* are illustrated on their particular totem poles. This shows the people that they have power and the authority over the land, they have fishing holes, the *ayuks* clearly identify who they are.

It tells the people that this land belongs to us. If you look at *Tenmigyet's ayuks* and know the *adawaak* of how the bear captured the woman, you know that happened where *Tenmigyet s* territory is today. That is how the *ayuks* are tied right back into the land.[11]

These *ayuks* are displayed on the regalia of the *Sigidim haanak'a* or *Simgigyet* and on other *wilp* property, such as *'am halitx, gwiis gan 'malaa,* and *am bilan.* However, the most important examples of *wilp* property displaying *wilp ayuks* are the *t'saan* or poles. As *Hanamuxw* testified:

> The pole indicates that you have a house. Without the pole it would be difficult to identify the House of *Hanamuxw* because your pole records the experiences of your house. They are the history of your house. The pole is evidence that *Hanamuxw's* house did exist, does exist and will continue to exist.
>
> Putting up a new pole is a way of reaffirming and confirming the *dax gyet* (power and authority) of *Hanamuxw*. It is the way of establishing that the property of *Hanamuxw* has not been abandoned, nor will it be in the future. It is a way of telling the other chiefs that the house is as strong as it was before, and that it will continue to exist because we have a fair number of people in our houses who will continue with the activities associated with the House of *Hanamuxw*, and who will ensure that it will exist in the future.[12]

"When the chief is planning to raise the pole," *Xamlaxyeltxw* testified, "it is very important that he thinks back to his territory. It is on the pole that he puts all the power and authority that he has. He puts all the crests of his *adawaak* on this pole. These poles show where the chief's jurisdiction is."[13]

Wams

The unbroken succession of ownership of the *lax'wiiyip* occurs through the passing of chiefly names that legally and spiritually connect the present generation to their ancestors. Besides *adawaaks* and *ayuks*, the *wilp* owns, as property, *wams*, or names, and these are significant as markers in the individual Gitxsan life cycle, especially with respect to the succession of the *Sigidim haanak'a* and the governance of *wilp* property. The inheritance of the *lax'wiiyip* on the death of the *Sigidim haanak'a* is renewed by the transfer of the chiefly *wam* and other named positions, duly witnessed by others of similar rank at various *li'ligit*. It is the name of the *Sigidim haanak'a*, according to Gitxsan tradition, which carries the *dax gyet* of the *wilp* and its genealogy can be traced back over the history of the Gitxsan people. In the most ordinary sense, a person's *wam* marks the transitional stages of a person's life. One is named at birth, as a young person, and perhaps later in life. As *Gyologyet* testified, "if he or she is in line of becoming a Chief a name is given to that person, and it is shown in the Feasting House just who are the people that are in line to become a Chief, as they are given an extra name."[14]

Some *wams* hold political influence, by virtue of the name itself. The highest-ranking *wam* in a *wilp* is the name of the *wilp*; for example, *Delgam'Uukw* is the highest ranking *wam* in the *Wilp* of *Delgam'Uukw*. Correspondingly, the person holding this name holds the most authority in the *wilp* and is referred to as the *Sigidim haanak'a*. To a large degree, the *Sigidim haanak'a* is the embodiment of the *wilp*. Similarly, there are names for members who act as spokespersons, and names specific to women and children. Not every person's name traditionally permits him or her to enter the *yukw*. One must hold a *wa'ayin wam* to sit at the *yukw*, as it is at the *yukw* that *wams* given to *wilp* members are validated.[15] Inheritance of *wams* and social positions specific to a particular *wilp* are reckoned through a matrilineal descent pattern, and rights to resources are attributes of political status fixed by *wams*, which in themselves are the property of the *wilp*. Those who hold the authority to allocate quotas for fish and determine the locations for hunting and trapping have obligations to ensure that there are enough resources for their kin — those related through marriage and those who are allied to the *wilp* by historic ties.

Lax'wiiyip

Gitxsan *lax'wiiyip*, especially resources sites — fishing sites, mountain passes, bear dens, and so on — are subject to control by the *wilp*. *Wilp lax'wiiyip* and the *ayuks* are the material foundation of the *wilp*, the basis for their social identity and the history of its members. As *Xhliimlaxha* testified, "In Gitxsan society the owner of *Xhliimlaxha's* territory are all the members of the house. This area is where they get their supply of food. *Xhliimlaxha* has been the owner since they discovered it, since they left Temlaham."[16]

The land is corporate property, in that the *wilp* as a unit holds a proprietary interest but lends rights of access to other groups. At the same time, the land holds incorporeal attributes, in that the Gitxsan belief structure compels them to view their relationship to the land in terms of the human-animal relationship and their history of encounters on it. These two aspects of property, the corporate and the incorporeal, are interwoven through the presence of the *Sigidim haanak'a,* who is the literal embodiment of the *wilp's* holdings and activities. The right to grant or withhold consent, or to use *wilp lax'wiiyip*, is contingent on the *Simgigyet* and *Sigidim haanak'a* having the public responsibility to see that the *lax'wiiyip* is used, its general fertility is maintained, and no one is left hungry. Those who are not members of one's *wilp* may be granted permission to use hunting territories and fishing stations. These persons are part of the *wilksiwitxw,* or from the spouse's kinship groups or *andimbanak*. Others may seek permission, which is usually granted subject to terms, which are usually some form of payment. As *Tenmigyet* wrote, "the fish are part of the rivers, as they have their own houses," and "it is not a *wilp's* right to deny another a livelihood." However, "the fishing station at site *Gwin k'alp* is the *Wilp* of *Tenmigyet*, and those people using it must adhere to the laws of the *Wilp* of *Tenmigyet*."[17] The user of the fishing site, berry patch, or hunting territory could make an on-the-spot contribution for the use (*daawxiis*), or the user was expected to present payment at a *yukw*. In response, the *wilp* would acknowledge the contribution and state to the community who has rights on their *lax'wiiyip*. Permission is sought from the *Sigidim haanak'a* to go onto the *wilp* territories to hunt, trap, gather, or fish. As *Gwiiyeehl* testified:

> After *Gitludahl* passed on and the name was passed on to me, I have the full authority to look after the place or to give permission to anyone that wants to go there and this includes the hunting, or trapping, or fishing, whatever *Gitludahl* had rights to give out. It's my responsibility to do it.

If I give anyone permission or they come to me and ask me if they want to go there, I will show them where to go and where to trap or where to hunt beaver or anything like that. We don't always go into the same place at the same year, we always move onto different territories.[18]

In essence, ownership of Gitxsan property is predicated on the ability of the *Sigidim haanak'a* to make appropriate decisions regarding the allocation of resources: first to *wilp* members; second to relations, including spouses and their respective families; and then to others who seek permission. The *Sigidim haanak'a* represents the *wilp's* right to exclusive possession of land and resources, and it is incumbent on the *Sigidim haanak'a* to be able to manage resource activities, including the labour necessary, and to provide political and spiritual leadership.

Together, the *adawaaks*, *ayuks*, and *wams* give the *wilp* the basis for its collectivity. The *adawaak* situates the *wilp* in Gitxsan territory in relationship to other *wilps*. The *adawaak* also defines the parameters of the *wilp's* territory that are directly associated with their history in the territory. The *ayuks*, or titles, that are carried into the *yukw* on ceremonial objects or *t'saan* illustrate to others present their specific *lax'wiiyip*. *Wams* reinforce the human-territorial relationship, either referencing the history directly, or through associating the person with a particular location on their *lax'wiiyip* and giving authority to those who have over the years demonstrated the ability to direct others and manage the resources on the *lax'wiiyip*.

Wilp boundaries have been fixed since the Gitxsan returned after the ice and snow retreated. Each *wilp*, through the recitation of its *adawaak*, can establish a proprietary interest in its *pteex lax'wiiyip*. Through a display of *ayuks*, each Gitxsan *wilp* can prove its respective boundaries and exclusivity to its particular *lax'wiiyip*. Moreover, the *ayuks* displayed on *t'saan* in any one generation list the relationships of the *wilp* to its *wilksiwitxw*, affirming territorial links through marriage and the proprietary resources, uses, and interests of the children. Since *huwilp adawaaks* describe the route *wilp* members took on their return to the *lax'wiiyip*, when the *lax'wiiyip* is spoken about at a *yukw*, it is referenced to named geographical, historical features, and specific events. For instance, "in our starvation *adawaak*," as *Tenmigyet* explained, "it describes in great detail our territory, the territorial names, the trails, and exterior boundaries, camp sites, bear dens; that is, where food is available."[19]

Where there are no distinguishing physical features, trees are blazed or rocks are piled, fixing the boundaries. As *Txaaxwok* testified:

An lii diks, it means that this landmark is where there is a post on the corner of a boundary, or a tree that has been blazed. A boundary can be a creek or a mountain that's never moved, or the creek that is not dry, a creek that runs all the time. They call this *an lii diks*. It does not move. They don't use anything that moves because it's a boundary. It's still the same today. They never changed. No one can change that.[20]

Tenmigyet clarified:

Where there are no other markers, trees are blazed, and we continually do this every time we come upon one. That is called *xsi gwin ixst'aat*, or we re-identify the mark by going over on top of the old blaze.

And as you get out of the tree line and start onto the mountain itself, there are piles of rocks used as markers along the ledges of the mountain. These rock piles are about 20, 30 feet apart and about two feet high. These markers are still up on the *Tsihl Gwellii* territory.[21]

Although the boundaries of each *lax'wiiyip* are fixed and specific *wilps* may lay claim to particular territories, a *wilp* may lose control over the ability to allocate resources on its *lax'wiiyip*. According to Gitxsan law, a *wilp* must forfeit the right to a resource location when one of its members is guilty of a capital crime, such as murder, rape, or larceny. In these cases, the *lax'wiiyip* may revert back to the original *wilp* only if the respondent is satisfied that the benefit received from the resource location has made up for the loss.[22] Also, if the *wilp* has difficulty covering the cost of funerals for its members, it will borrow from others, and these people, until the *wilp* is able to repay them, will hold one of the resource sites.[23]

Trespass

Property rights in all societies are guarded carefully, and Gitxsan laws of trespass require that the boundaries of the *wilp's lax'wiiyip* are known and permission is sought to hunt or fish on *wilp lax'wiiyip*. As *Tenmigyet* testified:

Territorial place names are announced in various ways. They are announced as an *adawaak* and they are announced when you bring your soup, your tea, your bread; they are announced and said this meat comes from, and it is specified which mountain or the territory it comes from. Each creek is mentioned. So in our rules and laws, we say that if you eat and digest the words, it is within your very soul.[24]

A hunter must respect the boundary lines, and others are obligated not to cross into another's *lax'wiiyip*. Trespass is equated with stealing. Before the *Lixs giigyet* were established in the region, a habitual trespasser could be killed for his behaviour. "So if you do that and they warn you," *Gwaans* testified, "and if you don't listen, they kill you right there. *Saagit* they call it."[25] When *saagit,* or justifiable homicide, occurs in Gitxsan society, it is usually as a result of habitual stealing of another *wilp's* resources.

"In the chiefs' houses we have our laws," *Gwis gyen* testified:

Each chief knows his own boundaries and this is held in their house. They know where their boundaries are and they know that no one could trespass over this boundary. They mention these boundaries in the feast hall, and they have chiefs and other Gitksan people listening to him, and they are witnessing this while he describes the boundary of his territory. Our people have our laws within the territories. Our law is that if a person has trespassed on your land and he has been warned and the third time he is caught there, he will be killed instantly. When this happens, the owner of the land will paint his face black.[26]

In this situation, one's kin cannot seek revenge, nor reimbursement: "There was a trespasser that went onto Nishga territory, and this trespasser was killed and was put back into the *T'aam Gins xhoux* (Sand Lake) and the people of *Tenmigyet* took the body and never said anything because they know that he was trespassing."[27]

While the Gitxsan acknowledge the seriousness of trespass, their means of redress are usually put aside if the person at fault goes to the *Sigidim haanak'a,* admits wrongdoing, and offers compensation. Similarly, the Gitxsan recognize the need to "pass through" another's *lax'wiiyip* in order to get to one's own, and provisioning during the course of a journey is permitted, but actively hunting in another's *lax'wiiyip* is forbidden:

When one of the family owns one territory up further than this territory here, then they walk on the territory of that other chief's to get to their territory. They don't go off of the trail and start hunting on that territory. They just keep walking until they get to their own territory.

They could shoot that animal on the trail, but they can't go in and hunt on that territory.[28]

It was expected, however, that the casual trespasser would recognize and compensate the owner of the *lax'wiiyip* at a *yukw* for extending this privilege, as X̱amlaxyeltxw testified:

> If this should happen, the person who trespassed apologizes to the chief then the chief would forgive this person. This would happen at a Feast, any kind of a Feast. This is done while the Feast is going on, in order for the people to hear.
>
> The trespasser will compensate the chief at the time when he apologizes in the Feast house.
>
> The Gitksan people don't apologize just to the Chief, because no one would know about it. In order for people to recognize what has happened and what's going on, they announce it in the Feast, and it is a correction that is made before the people.[29]

The *Sigidim haanak'a*, in the name of the *wilp*, gives permission to go onto the *lax'wiiyip* to fish, hunt, trap, or gather food. This right to grant or withhold consent is closely linked to the owner's responsibility to see that the land is well used, its fertility maintained, and that no one lacks basic subsistence. Those who are not members of the *wilp*, persons from one's father's side (*wilksiwitxw*) and from the spouses' kinship group (*andimbanak*) may seek and be granted permission to use the *lax'wiiyip* of the *wilp*. Persons who are not related to the *wilp* may ask permission as well, but access to a particular site or resource is usually for a specific and short period, and is announced at a *yukw*. The *Sigidim haanak'a* has the responsibility for the management of the *lax'wiiyip,* and all *wilp* members are obliged to seek permission to go onto the *lax'wiiyip*. It is the *Sigidim haanak'a*, in consultation with other *Sigidim haanak'a(s)*, who determines the quantities of fish and animals to be trapped or hunted each year.

"It's Gitksan law that we have to have permission," *Gyologyet* testified. "No one goes onto anybody's territory without getting permission from a head chief of the House of that territory, even if it's your own husband or your wife or your children. That's the law in Gitksan. Everybody has to ask permission, and be given permission."[30]

Anjok

The Gitxsan adhere to what is known as *anjok*, to be called out by the *Sigidim haanak'as* to use a resource in order to avoid trespass. This practice ensures that those interested in using a fishing site, hunting territory, or berry patch will have an opportunity to be given permission by the *wilp* to use a particular resource. "When it is time for fishing or berry picking," *Xhliimlaxha* testified, "the *Simgigyet* will invite the rest of the family. It is the traditional role of the *Simgigyet* to call first the family, then others who are related, the parents of the spouses, and lastly others who ask permission."[31]

After permission has been given, the *Sigidim haanak'as* provides a sign or symbol that illustrates to others that permission has been given. According to *Tenmigyet*:

> In earlier years the ladies of our House would make special straps that were colourful and visible. And if someone wanted to go onto the terri-tory they would ask permission from the chief, who controls the areas. They would give the chief something that came from their own terri-tory. They would exchange something for the permission to go to these berry patches, and they would have these strings tied to the baskets that they called *deex iiyasxw*. They were given these fancy coloured straps to identify that they already obtained permission from the chief.
>
> If a man came to the chief, and went to the territory without any member of our house accompanying him, then he would have to have some identification that said he had gained permission. This was done by a staff we call *k'aat'*. That's just a large staff they use to go up the mountain. And this staff would be coloured kind of a light blue colour and the way that this colour is obtained is from a lake we call in our language *T'amis maa'yaast*, and *maa'yaast* is trimming. If you stick a "stick" into the lake sediment and leave it for a few days, it would then change the colour of this cane, and this is the "staff" that we use for identification.[32]

Amnigwootxw

The *Sigidim haanak'as* regulate access to the *wilp's lax'wiiyip* according to established laws. *Wilp* members have access rights to resources on their *lax'wiiyip*, following the direction of the *Sigidim haanak'a*. Access rights are granted to non-*wilp* members, so that all Gitxsan people have access to their own, their father's, and their spouse's *wilp lax'wiiyip*. These rights, however, are contingent on proper use; if a marriage dissolves, so do the accompanying rights. This ensures that all Gitxsan people have access to the multitude of resources throughout the area. Under the principle of *amnigwootxw*, Gitxsan children have a right of access to their father's *lax'wiiyip* while their father is alive. After his death, they must ask permission, unless they are granted continued access by the *Sigidim haanak'a* of that *wilp*. *Xamlaxyeltxw* explained:

> *Amnigwootxw* is when the son travels with his father on his territory, and he will be with his father until his father dies. But after his father dies he does not say he owns this territory. He leaves and if he wants to go back there he has to get permission from the head chief of that territory before he goes back on to the territory where he and his father were before.[33]

Similarly, when one's daughter marries, the *Simgigyet* will grant the couple hunting privileges in their *wilp's lax'wiiyip* and the use of a fishing site:

> When a young man marries into the house of the young woman and they are both Gitksan people, what usually happens is the head chief of that woman's house gives a part of the land to this young man and he tells this young man to use this land to bring his children up on this land. And he also would give him a fishing site.
>
> If they happen to separate, then he has no rights to that territory. But if they go on living until his death, then he'll use that until his death. And then it goes back to his children.
>
> This is known as *yuugwilatxw*.[34]

When *Ax Gwin Desxw* married, for example, his wife's *wilp* gave their family access to a fishing site:

> The fishing hole is theirs, and she has some rights to it. And I have a responsibility to be with her. If we use the fishing hole it's under her direction. I also want to encourage my children to learn about fishing, and teach them our Gitksan laws. And before *Haalus* passed on he made sure we had a fishing hole.[35]

All *wilps* have the right to extend *amnigwootxw* rights to members outside their *wilp*, when an individual is brought in as a guardian to care for orphaned children and *wilp* property. As *Tenmigyet* stated:

> There are, in our house and all Gitksan houses, two types of *amnigwootxw*. Privileged *amnigwootxw* right is you don't have a name from our house but you're privileged to come on our territory through your father's side. This *amnigwootxw* I'm talking about now, Charlie Smith was the actual taking of a name from our house and using it to show control, jurisdiction, and ownership. If he did not obtain the name *Bii Lax ha* all other chiefs wouldn't have recognized his voice and he would have had no business talking about this house, he had no rights to be a care keeper, so in that sense he had to obtain the name *Bii Lax ha*.
>
> You might say that the type of *amnigwootxw* he was given was that he took the territory and held it in trust.[36]

In this form of *amnigwootxw*, the *wilp* extends the authority to make decisions regarding the management of the *lax'wiiyip* for surviving children. The guardian will be given a *wam* from the *wilp*, and is entrusted with its property. This person looks after the children and their tutelage, as well as the resources, transferring their inheritance back to them when they come of age. Similarly, *amnigwootxw* is extended to the heirs of a past *wilp*, allowing the *wilp* to show respect to that individual. In speaking of hunting privileges at a place called *Tsihl Gwellii*, *Tenmigyet* explained that his grandfather's children could trap there through *amnigwootxw*: "*Amnigwootxw* privileges are extended to them because they are the children of the former chief of our house."[37]

In this case, *amnigwootxw* was given not for fishing, but for hunting and trapping. Access to fishing sites usually ceases on the death of any *Sigidim haanak'a*. A fishing site usually has a guardian assigned to look after its defence and regulation. When the holder of the name passes on, the obligations and responsibilities associated with it pass to another. The new guardian of the fishing site, in consultation with the *Sigidim haanak'a*, is given the responsibility to allocate fish from the site in question. Priority is given to siblings and spouses of the immediate family, to ensure that the children are cared for. Permission is given to outsiders on a seasonal basis. "And at this fishing site we give *Niis Noohl amnigwootxw* to use the site," *Tenmigyet* explained, referring to the fishing site *Gwin k'alp*. "He requests permission every year to use this site."[38]

Amnigwootxw rights can be extended to others in recognition for services, or kindnesses offered. For example, when the *Wilp* of *Tenmigyet* could not afford the many funerals they were responsible for, the *Wilps* of *Haalus* and *Gwis gyen* paid for them. In return, the *Wilp* of *Tenmigyet* extended *amnigwootxw* privileges to them:

> *Gwis gyen* and his father did a great amount of work within our house. When people died, it was expensive. We were down at our lowest level, and his father *Ts'ii yee* did a lot of work for us and helped us quite a bit, so we consider *Gwis gyen* as *amnigwootxw*. In ancient history *Xsi gwin ixst'aat* in the *Tsihl Gwellii* area was always known *An t'ookxw*. And it simply means a banquet table. We welcomed them and have granted permission to them to come and use our territory.[39]

In all cases, *amnigwootxw* privileges exist for a specific term. When a non-*wilp* individual is given a name in order to care for orphans, *amnigwootxw* privileges are extended to that person until the rightful owners are given back their names. It is usual to extend continued *amnigwootxw* privileges to this person in recognition of service to the *wilp*.

Xkyeehl

A *Sigidim haanak'a* can grant another *wilp* or individual temporary access to specific locations through the principle of *xkyeehl*. Unlike *amnigwootxw* access, which is given as a reward, *xkyeehl* is given to the individual who approaches the *wilp* with some form of payment. *Tenmigyet* explained:

> *Xamlaxyeltxw* approached me with a really high priced article, which we use with our ceremonial *nax nox* in the feast hall. He has given me what we call an *am bilan*. That's part of the apron the chiefs use when they are in full regalia, and the *am bilan* has these little bells and the designs on it. The reason he gave me this is he wants to use one of our fishing sites. The members of the house will have to get together along with my mother, and we will then decide which of these fishing sites will best be suited to what he wants, whether he wants spring or sockeye salmon, then a decision will have to be made on which area he wants to use. This is called *xkyeehl*, it is done through the *yukw*.[40]

The granting and the acknowledging of *xkyeehl* at a *yukw* formalizes the *wilp's* authority over the *lax'wiiyip* in question. Such practices publicly affirm the authority of the *Sigidim haanak'a* to grant permission as well as the *wilp's* right of exclusivity. Thus, people unrelated to the *wilp* can acquire rights to resources or locations or labour through payment at a *yukw*. In practice, the Gitxsan hold rights against each other, and owe obligations to one another. Tenure and ownership arises, and is maintained, through the fulfillment of obligations to others, in combination with title to the land itself.

The Right to Alienate the Lax'wiiyip

The boundaries of *wilp lax'wiiyip* have been fixed by the Creator, and the resources on these territories are given to the *wilps* to use as their table. The *wilp* is entrusted with the management of these territories as long as they are respectful. Part of this obligation is to provide for the funeral of the departed *Sigidim haanak'a* in a manner befitting the honour of the departed. There are some situations in which another *wilp* must sponsor the funeral, and a lien is placed on the *wilp's lax'wiiyip* until this debt is repaid. When it is necessary to compensate another *wilp* for the loss of a life, either by accident or homicide, the *lax'wiiyip* is given to other *wilp* as compensation, until their hearts are full (as determined by the recipient *wilp*). Eventually, this *lax'wiiyip* reverts back to the original *wilp*. This is one of the prerogatives of the *Sigidim haanak'a*.

To uphold the honour of the *wilp*, the incoming *Sigidim haanak'a* must be able to afford the responsibilities of the office, among which is the obligation to pay for the funeral of the late *Sigidim haanak'a* and requisite memorials in subsequent years. Though most of the obligations fall on the shoulders of the new *Sigidim haanak'a*, the *wilp* will pool its resources to sponsor the various ceremonies and feasts that accompany the funeral and memorials. In some cases, these expenses are paid for by one's *wil'na t'ahl* or *wilksiwitxw*. In these situations, one's *wilp* owes a debt, and until the debt is paid, the creditor's *wilp* may hold part of the debtor's *lax'wiiyip*. As *Txaaxwok* explained:

> *Sduutxw'm Lax ha* is the owner as I stated before. Anytime when these people were working together on a funeral feast, they were helped by *Waiget* [of the Fireweed] with all the expenses in the feast.
>
> The *Xsi maxhla saa Giibax* territory was turned over to *Waiget*. They turned it over to him because that's the only way they can thank these people.

The Fireweed put up the feast and the Wolf and the Frog Clan were seated. All three clans were there to witness and approve what was put into the feast.

Waiget had become the *dax yuk dit lax yip*, the caretaker of the territory. This is what was approved at the feast.[41]

In keeping with First Nations' principles of restorative justice, if a feud between two persons escalates and one is killed, the *wilp* of the offending party could transfer some *lax'wiiyip*, until their hearts are full. Basically, this means that when there is *mix k'aax*,[42] peace made between two *wilps*, over the wrongful death of one of its members, restitution must be made in the form of the transfer of a portion of the offending *wilp's* hunting area, fishing station, or trapping line until such time as the other *wilp* believes that restitution has been made. *Gwaans* gave an example in his testimony at trial:

> *Hanamuxw* acquired the fishing site *An si bilaa* after *'Niitsxw* was killed. *Ha'atxw* was trying to marry his sister, *'Niitsxw's* sister. *'Niitsxw* refused to let *Ha'atxw* marry his sister, and *Ha'atxw* killed him. There was a peace made between them, *Gawa gyanii* and the fishing site of *An si bilaa* was given to *Hanamuxw*.[43]

Antgulilbix related, similarly, that the *Wilps* of *Antgulilbix* and *Tsibasaa* were awarded the territory beyond the ridge outside Kispiox as *xsiisx*, or compensation, for the killing of *Yal*:

> At the end . . . where the ridge is, is their boundary, but the other side of the ridge was given to both *Antgulilbix* and *Tsibasaa* as a compensation because *Yal* was murdered on the ice where *Xsagangaxda* runs into the Skeena River.
>
> There was a tree standing there and they would smear this tree with blood. The crest on this tree is a sun. That's the *Gisk'aast* crest, and that tree represents the compensation that was given in exchange for the blood [of *Yal*] and it won't be taken back from us until the end of the world.[44]

Besides being compensated for the accidental or intentional death of a person, a *wilp* could acquire territories as a result of inter-community raiding and warfare. In his commissioned evidence, *Lelt* explained the aftermath of the failed raid of the Stikine:

The big chief of the Stikine waved the wings of the birds of Meziaden. And as he waved them, he said, there will be peace. This will be your land, we will not return here, we will return to our own village and there will be no more wars.

Then the Stikine person waved his hand, saying "this will be your land." "This will be your land." He waved his hand some more. And he blew the eagle down. The eagle down floated all around.

Xsiisx. They compensated us for the killing of *Txawok* and *Ligigalwil.*[45]

Even if death was accidental, as happened at Kispiox, the offending *wilp* was quick to offer compensation:

This happened at Kispiox. The folks from Glen Vowell were pretending to attack Kispiox, they pretended to have a war and they captured one of the chiefs, from the house of *Ma'uus.* They took him away to Glen Vowell. On the next night the people of Kispiox were preparing to attack Glen Vowell and take back the one that was captured. After they left the ladies also decided to go. The ladies got guns that were also emptied of bullets. Then they started out over the ice to Glen Vowell.

And not far from *Gwin o'op* they met men from the House of both *Dawamuxw's* and *'Niista huuk's* and his brother, *Laan.* The ladies pretended to shoot him. They just said, "*guxw, guxw, guxw.*" One young lady that came along with them pointed the gun to the side of this man and it went off. The man said slowly, "You — you shot me," and then he flopped down really slow.

The *wilp* of the young lady who shot the man sent a little boy to spy on the house of the man who died. When the little boy came back to their house, he said the other house was singing their war song. They were preparing to strike back.

The Chief had put on all his regalia — his blankets, head dress and got his rattle; and he went to the other house. When the Chief went into the house, he sang his *Xsinaahlxw* (breath song) with his rattle in his hand.

After the breath song, he spoke to the Chiefs of the man that was shot and he told them he was willing to give part of his house's hunting ground to them. So everything was settled.

He gave the land, the hunting ground after the breath song, as *xsiisx,* compensation.[46]

Although it appears that the *wilp* may alienate its territory as a means of set-tling or preventing a blood feud, the *lax'wiiyip* in question is still owned by the *wilp* that offered it. This portion of territory will be returned to its own-ers when the other *wilp* has determined that the loss that occurred has been forgotten. The *lax'wiiyip* does not belong to individuals, but is held by the *Sigidim haanak'a* for the benefit of all *wilp* members; it can only be alienated under certain circumstance, and only then for particular periods.

The *Sigidim haanak'a* and Governance Principles

The *Simgigyet* or *Sigidim haanak'a* represent all *wilp* members' rights of owner-ship, and are responsible for directing and safeguarding the fruits of the land, the labour of the people, and the knowledge necessary for each *wilp* member to attain an appropriate standard of living. In accordance with Gitxsan rules of succession, almost anyone in a *wilp* has the opportunity to become a *Si-gidim haanak'a*. Although it is more likely that one will inherit the position from a close relative, it takes more than just being in line.

The *Sigidim haanak'a* is responsible for the management of *wilp* property, and so must interweave aggressive exclusivity with the conferring of rights of access on others, based on reciprocity. The *Sigidim haanak'a* must ensure that *wilp* members have enough for food, to cover the costs of running the fishery, to cover the *wilp's* trade, and provide for collective obligations. The *Sigidim haanak'a* must also ensure that *wilp* needs, in conjunction with other *huwilp*, do not damage the breeding stock of plants, fish, or animals. In the seasonal round of hunting, trapping, and berry-picking, it is the responsibility of the *Sigidim haanak'a*, in conference with other *Simgigyet* or *Sigidim haanak'a*, to direct when and where *wilp* members hunt, trap, or gather. In consultation with *wilp* members, the *Sigidim haanak'a* then allocates access to resources to the spouses of the *wilp* members in order that the children are cared for.

One's father's *wilp* reciprocates, allocating or granting permission to their resources. Although property and rank come from the mother's family, the father's family occupies an important place in Gitxsan society. It is the respon-sibility of the father's family at a birth to provide the cradle; at a death, it is the father's descendants who look after the body, dig the grave, and provide the coffin. During a *wilp* member's early life, it is the task of the father's family to teach the *ayooks,* and it is the duty of a father's family to provide the money necessary to validate the names a person receives over his or her lifetime. During the father's life, permission is sought through the father, and afterward permission is granted by the *Sigidim haanak'a*. This establishes a pattern of reciprocity that continues throughout the father's lifetime. At the father's death, though a person is enveloped by the father's *wil'na t'ahl*, the extended matrilineal family, the contribution of the father's family is never forgotten.

Wilp resources are allocated to others for good deeds, or one may draw upon them through payment. This is expressed in the day-to-day routines of *wilp* members, relatives, spouses, and non-*wilp* members asking permission from the *Sigidim haanak'a* to go onto *wilp lax'wiiyip* to hunt, trap, fish, or gather berries, and it is incumbent on the *Sigidim haanak'a* to know the capacity of the *wilp's* resources in order that thoughtful advice be given to *wilp* members. If *wilp* members disregard the word of the *Sigidim haanak'a* and over-hunt or over-fish, the fish or animals have the right to withdraw from the *wilp's lax'wiiyip*.[47] Each *wilp* member must respect the authority of the *Sigidim haanak'a*, as she alone bears the cost of the animals' withdrawal from the territory. She must ensure that respect is afforded the animals in that *wilp* members are expected not to overkill them, to thank them for submitting, and to look after their remains in order that they, too, may be reincarnated.[48]

Succession

The *dax gyet* of the *wilp* — its power and authority — is contingent on it being able to fulfill its ritual obligations at the passing of one of its members and at the succession of the *Sigidim haanak'a*. It is therefore incumbent on the current or incoming *Sigidim haanak'a* or *Simgigyet* to be able to ensure that the *wilp*, individually and collectively, is able to sustain its members, to respect the animals and fish, and meet their ritual and ceremonial obligations. The transfer of the *lax'wiiyip* on the death of the *Sigidim haanak'a* is renewed by the transfer of the chiefly name, duly witnessed by others of similar rank at a *yukw*. At the time of a *Sigidim haanak'a* or *Simgigya's* impending death, members of the *wilp* and *wil'na t'ahl* congregate to discuss who is going to be the successor.

"It is only when the chief dies," *Xamlaxyeltxw* testified, "that the name of the head chief is passed on. The head chief is responsible for the house and it is he who has the power for that house, and the only time they can put this name on somebody is when the chief dies. When the new chief takes the head chief's name, then he is responsible for everything in that house."[49]

The qualities of the person chosen for the position must be more than just being in the line of succession and being able to manage and afford the obligations of the *yukw*. As *Hanamuxw* testified, the elders must have observed that a potential *Sigidim haanak'a* is able to "handle situations, and I think one of the most important qualities that they need to see in you as the future candidate for a chief is whether you accepted your creator, the protection that he gives you, the guidance, the wisdom that he provides for you and that you respect your elders at all times."[50]

At the conclusion of the meetings, a successor is asked to assume the responsibilities of *Sigidim haanak'a*. Those in attendance endorse the new chief, and the community begins funeral preparations for the departed one. With the inheritance of the *Sigidim haanak'a's wam* comes the inheritance of *wilp* property:

> All the Chiefs get together, they come with their regalia on, and they sing their *limxoo'y* (dirge songs). They speak to the dead Chief. The Chiefs say all what he has done during his lifetime, we repeat his *adawaak*, and name all the feasts that he has put on. We call the new Chief out by her baby name, asking for her to come in. We ask her to see her grandfather buried.[51]

As *Hanamuxw* testified at trial, when she assumed the hereditary title of *Hanamuxw*, her elders addressed her with this statement:

> "*Hlaa niin xsi gyalatxwit dim ant guuhl hli dax gyets dip niye'en. Dim guudinhl wa midim'y ama gya'adihl Lax yip.*" This roughly means that you are the one that has been selected to take the land that was your inheritance, to hold it, and to take care of it.
>
> This means the land that your forefathers had, that includes the regalia, the *adawaak*, the pole, the resources on the land, the name *Hanamuxw*, and the right to use that name within the Gitksan territory, and that you are the one that has been selected to take the land that was your inheritance, to hold it, and to take care of it. This also means the right to use the authority of the chief, which includes providing leadership for the people, the *Gisk'aast* as well as the other clans in Gitsegukla. It means preserving the history of the house. It means taking care of the present, and always with the idea that you link it with the future. It means having the right to assist not just the people in your own house, but everyone in your community if they need help. It means going to other levels of authority whenever you need to negotiate with them to

take care of the needs of the people, or it may mean going to neighbouring nations and negotiating with them issues that deal with the Indian problems, or it may mean offering suggestions as to how these can be solved. It also means that you as the chief have the responsibility of training the younger members of your family so that all the traditions, all the customs, all the rituals within your house are maintained. So in a sense the chief is also the teacher for the younger people as well as a counselor, as well as a spiritual leader.[52]

At the *Hidinsim Getingan Yukw* — headstone or totem pole raising feasts, usually held a year after the passing of the *Sigidim haanak'a* — the new chief is fully endorsed by Gitxsan society. At a series of *yukws*, the hosting *wilp* displays its *dax gyet* by asking other *huwilp* to endorse the new *Sigidim haanak'a*. It is at this time that the *Gal dim algyak*, the speaker for the *wilp*, introduces the *Sigidim haanak'a* to the community, leading her to the seat in the *yukw* of the departed *Simgigyet*. The *Sigidim haanak'as* from other *wilps* call out her new name as she passes, saying, *"ee dim uma yees"* (on the breath of your ancestor). During the course of events, the *Gal dim algyak* calls out the names of the boundaries of the *wilp's lax'wiiyip*, and the *adawaaks* of the *wilp* are re-enacted. Similarly, the *wilp's ayuks* are either recounted or performed, using the *wilp's* songs and dances. The other *Sigidim haanak'as* in attendance present their *adawaaks* in response to the presentation of the *Sigidim haanak'a's* symbols of authority. This presentation constitutes a re-enactment of the time the Gitxsan were cast out of *T'am Lax amit*, and their return to the region after the ice left.

The *adawaak* told by the new *Sigidim haanak'a* at this time indicates to the community her knowledge of the *wilp's lax'wiiyip*, its history, its *ayuks* and its inter-relations to other *huwilp*. Accuracy is imperative, as the *adawaak* is a description of the property of the *wilp*. In addition, it is within the ritual of the *yukw* that the *dax gyet* of the *Sigidim haanak'a* is refuted or affirmed. *Ax Gwin Desxw* explained:

> The authority is within that particular house group, and the main host of that feast is mainly the hereditary chief of that house who is the major decision-maker along with his house members. They are the ones that are in main control of the feast. What the chief is doing is that he is demonstrating publicly in that feast to the other chiefs that he has invited, that he knows the laws that he has to follow for that particular

feast, and he is demonstrating publicly that he has land, that he has fishing holes, that he has power, that he has wealth and that he owns the land; and these are my other members of my immediate house. He is publicly telling all the people in that feast hall, that this is who I am, I am a chief, I am a high chief, and this is my authority.[53]

It is important that the witnessing *Sigidim haanak'as* and *Simgigyets* pay close attention to what is recited at this time. This is as *Gitludahl* has said:

> The Chiefs are there and they witness everything that is done during the feast. They see that everything is done properly, and that we speak about what is to be done. And that is why all the chiefs are there to witness the feast. If everything is done the right way, they say they are glad they attended and witnessed the feast. They are all satisfied. If I say anything wrong or something is given away that does not belong to *Gitludahl* or in any of our territories, one of the chiefs is going to stand up and speak up and say this is not true.[54]

If the new *Sigidim haanak'a* makes an error, it is up to the chiefs witnessing the *yukw* to tell the *'Nii dil* (the sponsor of the incoming *Sigidim haanak'a*), who will, in turn, inform the new *Sigidim haanak'a*. The new *Sigidim haanak'a* will rectify the error at a subsequent *yukw* called to correct the mistake: "You stand up and speak and mention that this is not quite right (either a boundary, *adawaak,* or *ayuk*) and then it is noted by the people, by whoever's House that is putting on the feast. It is noted what you objected to, and so the next time you put up your feast what others have objected to, it is then corrected."[55]

At the various *yukws* associated with the funeral of the departing *Simgigyet* and the investiture of the incoming *Sigidim haanak'a* is the public display of the *wilp's* possessions and prosperity. As *Gyologyet* explained, this *yukw* is to

> get the people together to witness the giving of the name of the deceased chief to another. Of course, there is a lot of people that we ask to work for the family, especially at the Burial Feast; and even at a Totem Pole Feast. There are people that are invited and asked to do certain work. Like at the burial, we have to get people to dig the grave; at a totem pole raising, we have to have people dig a hole to put the totem pole in, so all these little things that are done, we have to pay them for this. The other

chiefs would witness that the family has paid for whatever is necessary.

The most important part of a Feast is when a name is given to a chief and the authority of what that name stands for, and what it holds. The names of the House's fishing sites, the trap lines on the territory, these are things that have to be told to the people every time there is a new chief.

At every Feast there has to be an *adawaak* given. When one person dies in a House, the *adawaak* of that House is told in the Feast House. The *adawaak* tells how they get their names, their songs and their fishing places, where they hold their trap lines, their hunting places, and their berry picking places; these are all told at a Feast, so that everyone knows and understands where these people have their territory and how they get their names. This is the importance of a Feast. We change our names four times before we become a chief. So with all these changes, we have to have a Feast so that these changes may be recorded, as names are also given to others in the House.

In the name of the *wilp* the new *Sigidim haanak'a* affirms the boundaries to their *lax'wiiyip* and their claims to the *ayuks*. At the *yukws* associated with the succession of the *Sigidim haanak'a,* the *adawaak* is recited and the *nax nox* of the *wilp* performed. In response to this display of *dax gyet,* other *huwilp* in attendance endorse the new *Sigidim haanak'a* and *wilp's* claim of ownership by responding with their *adawaak* and displaying their *nax nox* and *ayuks*. Throughout the life of a *Sigidim haanak'a*, she will be called upon to witness other new *Sigidim haanak'a's* initiations, to bury other *wilp* members, to help the *wilp*, the community, and look after the *wilp's* property (*lax'wiiyip, wams, ayuks* and *adawaaks*). During her later years, she will be actively grooming another to take her place when she passes on.[56]

Dispute Resolution

Those who show the promise of leadership early in their life have their ears pierced in order that they neither hear bad things about others nor engage in gossip that will hurt another. This witnesses to others that they were being trained to be impartial, and were receiving additional training in spiritual matters to prepare their mind and body to take on the responsibilities of being the *Xsgooim Sigidim haanak'a*.[57] One of these additional responsibilities is the ability to mediate disputes. The most common internal *wilp* dispute among the Gitxsan is over the inheritance of a name. If the ailing *Sigidim haanak'a* has not clearly identified her successor, her choice is not supported by *wilp* consensus, or the *Sigidim haanak'a* passes away unexpectedly, those making the choice may disagree among themselves as to who will inherit the position. If they are unable to resolve the matter among themselves, the *wilp* can either announce at the *Sigidim haanak'a's* funeral that they are burying the name, or they may call on other *Simgigyets* and *Sigidim haanak'a* to mediate a resolution. *Gyologyet* related an example:

> *Miluulak* died, one of the head chiefs of the *Gisk'aast*, and they had to have a person to take her name.
>
> At that time there was the two people who could be the chief. They both felt that they ought to be the person to take the name of *Miluulak*. It was not settled by the day of the funeral amongst the *Miluulak's* House. The family was still pulling for one, or the other.
>
> This is when the chiefs of the different clans, the Frog and the Fireweed, were called to *Miluulak's* House. The head chiefs, who were called to the House, were asked to settle this. So after a lengthy discussion, we settled that one of the people would take the name of *Miluulak*, and the other would look after the territory.[58]

This panel of *Sigidim haanak'as* works with the *wilp* to find a solution all can agree on. The conflict, as well as the resolution, is brought into the open at the inauguration of the new *Sigidim haanak'a*. "All this had to be told at the Feast of how the family disagreed and how it could not be settled," *Gyologyet* explained at trial. "It was also told that they called on the chiefs of the different clans to settle it for them and that they had all agreed, the family of *Miluulak's*, and the *wil'na t'ahl* agreed with that. This was all said and settled in the Feasting House."[59]

Similarly, a *Simgigyet* in the role of a *'nii dil,* uses his knowledge to assist others in resolving conflicts, as *Tenmigyet* recounted:

> I will speak of how my role as a *'Nii dil* was when there was a dispute concerning the area around Boulder Creek. *Sinankxws* came to me when there was a meeting in Hazelton about this area and it was said that this area was theirs. So I spoke to her *'Nii dil*. I then rose at the meeting, and said the Boulder Creek area actually belonged to them, was true.

Also the late *Ax tii hiikw* was in a similar situation when the *Genada* was trying to put a chief's name on a non-Indian. *Lelt* said it's up to our *'Nii dil* to say, and then my grandfather, *Ax tii hiikw*, stood up and he says "No, it cannot be held by this person," and it was then stopped.[60]

In other situations, including larger problems between communities, the *Simgigyets* and *Sigidim haanak'as* are "pulled out" to a series of meetings to resolve either a local concern or to forward a concern to an outside community. Again, *Tenmigyet* testified:

> *Sisixek* means that we have to involve other chiefs, the *wilxsi leks* and others. Then you do *sisixsek*, that mean "you pull out the chiefs," the forerunning chiefs, to make the decisions. This is not in the Feast Hall, but when you have a dispute you would go to certain chiefs and ask them to help you in these decision-making roles. We usually "pull them out" from all the houses. We try to pull from every house in each of the villages. At times we go to the Wet'suwet'en in Hagwilget, so everybody is involved.[61]

All the *Simgigyets* and *Sigidim haanak'as* are bound to consult with others. "Consultation starts at your house level and then it would go to your *wil'na t'ahl* and to your *wilksiwitxw*," according to *Hanamuxw*. "Next, the village must decide if the action that has been proposed is right. This involves all the clans."[62]

As explained by *Ax Gwin Desxw*, the *Simgigyets* and *Sigidim haanak'as* have the final word:

> Generally there is a fair bit of discussion on certain issues. Different individuals, whether they are young or older, make their views known publicly, and in some cases where things are very difficult, the chiefs will listen and if things are not going properly, they will speak, and then they overrule what the younger people are saying. And even the council, they are the last ones to speak, they say the final word, and nobody else speaks after that, and then the discussion is finished. The Chiefs have the final word.[63]

Management Responsibilities

The *Sigidim haanak'a* directs and protects *wilp* resources for use by its members, the spouses of its members, the member's father's family, and, lastly, all others who ask to use the property. All Gitxsan therefore have access to their own *wilp's lax'wiiyip*, the *lax'wiiyip* of their father's *wilp*, and the *lax'wiiyip* of their spouse's *wilp*. The *Sigidim haanak'a*, as steward, controls not only the members of her *wilp*, but access to her *wilp's* resources by related *huwilp*. According to Richard Daly, the *Sigidim haanak'a* exercises a proprietary right toward the land vis-à-vis the claims of other groups and simultaneous reciprocal stewardship vis-à-vis the land and creatures who live on it.[64] Access to the resources of *wilp* members are safeguarded by the *Sigidim haanak'a's* authority to manage their claims as well as give voice to the rights protecting them against the claims of others. It is expected that *wilp* members and non-*wilp* members alike will heed the word of the *Sigidim haanak'a*, for she has equal obligations to the animals, plants, and fish who reside on the territories and in the streams, and she, in the name of the *wilp*, will bear the burden of shame if the animal, plants, and fish disappear from the *lax'wiiyip*.

The Fishery

The *Sigidim haanak'a*, again in the name of the *wilp*, organizes and directs the fishery, and manages hunting and trapping on the *lax'wiiyip* in accordance with selective harvesting principles. If a *wilp* takes too many fish in one season, they run the risk of causing other *wilps* as well as neighbouring communities upstream, to not meet their quotas. It is the responsibility of the *Sigidim haanak'a*, in consultation with *wilp* members, to determine the number of fish needed.[65] Members are asked to review their larders to determine their needs for the upcoming year, based on their consumption in the previous year. Before allocating the *wilp's* need, the *Sigidim haanak'a* must ensure that debts from trading owed by *wilp* members, and the costs associated with running the fishery, are met. As *Tenmigyet* explained:

> She asks me, "How much do you need?" I tell her how much I need, how much my sister needs, and how much my brothers need. This is calculated along with what is needed for our trade and what might be needed as the payment for the equipment that we will be using.

In late August we congregate at the smoke house and my mom would have a tarp laid out here, a bright red tarp, and all the fish that was processed all summer would be divided and counted into bundles of 40, we call *k'i'yhl luuks*.

People give us things, like, for instance, the net was supplied by one of the Kitwancool members, and in return he wants some of these prize fish, prized *huxws* (Spring Salmon); and in the case of the boat, that boat we use, *T'ewelasxw's* boat, the stern kicker itself is supplied by our minister, Reverend McLeod, and in turn we have to pay him back. Usually, we try to deal with these outside things first before we accommodate our own needs.[66]

Hunting

The *Sigidim haanak'a* can only allow *wilp* members to take the amount of fish or game that they need, and no more. Other *Sigidim haanak'a* consult with each other in order that they know what the needs of their *wilp* members are to make sure that they do not deplete the stock. After the fishery has shut down in early fall, hunting and trapping is planned.

"We look after the land by using it," *Tenmigyet* testified:

If you don't hunt and fish your territories, the salmon, the mountain goats, the beaver, and the ground-hogs won't stay round. If you are not active, they just go away. We've always taken just what we needed, and then we protect the life cycle of the rest. We have always limited our hunting to fall and winter, when the young are no longer dependent on their mothers. We guard the spawning beds, we burned the berry patches to keep them healthy and productive. We even used controlled burning to get rid of the insects which kill off the trees.[67]

Gitxsan must follow the rules of the hunt and share what has been taken. According to the *Adawaak 'Wiihloots*, if Gitxsan people quarrel over food, a *siyehl widit*, a curse, will be brought onto their *wilp*. When the law of respect and sharing is broken, *tss'uu wijix*[68] will occur, or the animals and fish will disappear, leaving the *wilp* to starve.[69] The laws of the hunt and sharing were enacted to ensure that hunting parties adhered to specific codes of behaviour, and their respective *Simgigyets* were responsible for ensuring that the laws are followed. Similarly, the laws of sharing reflect an age grade that looks after the elders first, then families with small children. As property flows through the matrilineal line, brothers who hunt and fish will supply their sisters with food, and the sisters, in turn, will support their brother's political roles. Husbands and wives are looked after by their own *wilp*. *Tenmigyet* clarified the law as it would apply to a mountain goat:

> The first one is we decide on how many animals we are going to kill, depending on the number in the hunting group, and then we don't over kill.
>
> The second one is never kill a mother . . . with young ones.
>
> The next one is the animal has to be cleaned where it was killed. *Gaak*, the raven, who announced the kill, has to be fed.
>
> After field dressing, the cuts, the hide, whatever that we do not need, has to be burned, in order that we satisfy our belief in reincarnation.
>
> The fifth one would be the actual roasting of the head of the goat, which is pointed towards the mountains that provided this goat, as thanks.[70]

"I will show them where to go and where to trap, or hunt beaver," *Gitludahl* said. "We don't always go to the same place in the same year, we always move onto different territories.[71]

Gitxsan hunters, on returning to their village, further divide what has been killed and share first with their elders, their *wilxsileks* (the plural of *wilksiwitxw*, one's father's side), and those to whom they have special obligations. *Ayooks* of *Naa hlimoot'* direct the Gitxsan to respect each other and the environment, and the *Simgigyets* must inform each other of their hunting plans, as *Txaaxwok* explained:

> The three clans that lived at Kisgagas, the Fireweed, Frog Clan and the Wolf clan, decided to meet with each other to discuss how to use the area called *Luu skadakwit* for hunting. In this area there is moose, bear, ground squirrels, and at the lake called *Dam ana koots*, there is beaver. The meeting was called to decide what animals were to be hunted in this area, and how many would be killed.[72]

Trap Lines

In order to protect their historic interests after the Crown asserted sovereignty, and in keeping with their commitment to comply with the Queen's law, the Gitxsan registered their trap lines with the province and have been vigilant in transferring them on the death of a *Sigidim haanak'a*. They also have abided by the requirement to take inter-*wilp* property disputes to the residing Justice of the Peace, who for most of the past century has been the local Indian Agent. As *Gyologyet* testified:

> In 1935, Joseph Danes died. He was *Gyologyet* at that time and while he was alive he would go onto our territory and hunt and trap. Sometimes Joseph Danes would take Tommy Muldoe (from the *Wilp* of *Spookw'* and at this time his name was *Madiigim gyetu*) up onto our territory and they would trap together. After Joseph Danes died in 1937 Tommy Muldoe claimed this trapping area as his own. My mother heard about this and went to Captain Mortimer, the Indian Agent in Hazelton, charging Tommy Muldoe with trespassing.
>
> My family went to the hearing called at the Indian Agent office in Hazelton and it was not settled that year. The next year Tommy Muldoe again tried to claim the trap line on our territory as his. So my grandmother went to the *Wilp* of *Spookw'* and said, "You are not going to own that territory." They said, "It does not belong to *Gyologyet*, but it belongs to all the Houses." So we went to the Court again. This time all head chiefs from the different clans came to the hearing. Now all the chiefs that spoke said that this territory belonged to *Gyologyet* and their other Houses in their *Wi'nat'ahl*. The chiefs pointed out to the Indian Agent and they mentioned all the creeks that they knew were on that territory and told who held the creeks, and they are from *Gyologyet's*, like *Kwamoon*, *Hlho'oxs*, and *Mediik*. They told Mr. Muldoe that he had his own House and own territory, that he was not supposed to be on *Gyologyet's* territory. So that is when it was settled then and he did not try again to take over and own our territory.[73]

However, as *Gyologyet* continued, some Gitxsan have trespassed on others' territories when registering their trap lines:

Mr. W. Danes, who is the son of Joseph Danes, has a trap line on the territory called *Win skahl Guuhl*. In order to get to his trap line he needs to go through our territory, Also, occasionally he will ask permission to go and trap on that place. We always give permission as he is the son of the late Joseph Danes who was *Gyologyet* before me. However, Mr. W. Blackwater, one of our neighbours has a trap line that overlaps on our territory. The same happened when Mr. W. Wilson registered his trap line in Smithers; he partly registered his trap line on our territory. These events happened because the Provincial Fish and Wildlife Department insisted that everyone register their trap lines on their traditional territories or lose them.[74]

However, as *Txaaxwok* testified, "My father held the name of *Waiget*, and was the registered owner of the trap line on the territory called *luu ska'yan't*. When he passed on there was a caretaker for the territory for a while and then the name of *Waiget* was passed to Elsie Morrison." Speaking of his territory, he continued: "Mr. John Robinson was the holder of the registered trap line in *Txaaxwok's* territory as he was *Txaaxwok* before me. Just before he died he transferred the trap line to me, and the person that replaces the chief is to manage resources on the territory."[75]

Ecological Concerns

The *Simgigyets* believe that the animals and birds have been placed in particular locations for their benefit, and that part of their responsibility is to be actively engaged on the territories. "The other Chiefs taught me how to hunt and to trap," *Txaaxwok* related, "and to go to certain places at different times of the year for different animals, how to learn to use the territory, and not to abuse it."[76]

When you are out on the territory hunting or trapping you are not alone. There may be 10 to 15 other chiefs and sub-chiefs there as well, like myself, managing their territory. We all talk to each other as we have to know where everyone has been trapping, where they have been hunting, and what animals have been taken. We have to report this to each other to know what animals have taken from the different groups and locations each year.[77]

Similarly, it is important that every few years the berry grounds be burnt, in order to preserve the quality and quantity of the berries. "The berries usually come back about three years later after we burn it," *Sak Higookw* explained.[78]

The obligation of the Gitxsan toward the animals extends beyond just making sure that they do not over-fish, hunt, or trap. It is incumbent on the *Sigidim haanak'a* to ensure that the environment is conducive for the animals to continue with their lives. Besides directing the fishery from April until late September or early October, the *Sigidim haanak'as* are also responsible for the environment of the salmon. "We guard the salmon spawning beds, as you can not walk on where fish eggs are laid," *Ax Gwin Desxw* explained. "It is important that you clean out the trees that have fallen into the streams. You respect the salmon and do not play with salmon bones, or make fun of them. And you return the remains to the river."[79]

Li'ligit

It is at the various *li'ligit*, or feasts, that Gitxsan *huwilp* come together to acknowledge their history, the continuation of the *wilp*, the bounty that has come from the *lax'wiiyip*, and to endorse the current business. It is incumbent on the *Sigidim haanak'a* to ensure that all *wilp* members have surpluses available to fulfill the *wilp's* collective obligation to host or contribute to a *yukw*.

There are *li'ligit* for naming, for the first kill of a young man, for marriage, for adoption, for divorce, for the settlement of disputes and the wiping-off of shame, for funerals, for the succession of a *Sigidim haanak'a* or *Simgigyet*, and for the raising of a pole or a headstone. There are also ceremonies of *Xai mooksisim* (first snowfall) and the *Skoog'm hon* (first salmon ceremony) that honour the bounty that comes from the *lax'wiiyip*, specifically recognizing the willingness of the animals and salmon to submit themselves to the Gitxsan as food.

In December, or after the first snowfall, the *Laxgibuu pteex* hosts the *Xai mooksisim Laxgibuu*. The *Laxgibuu's 'Nii dil* (sponsor) calls on the *Laxgibuu pteex* to put on a feast for the villagers, as it is the time in which the footprints of the wolves are seen in the snow. This feast, the *Xai mooksisim Laxgibuu*, is a means for the Gitxsan to give thanks to all the animals. All the foods that come from the territories are served, and the places they have come from are named. In April, when the Spring Salmon return, the first salmon caught is placed on a special mat and carefully cooked. Pieces of this fish are given to

the other villagers, and as one receives this fish, one gives thanks to the Creator for providing it. In this ceremony, the *Skoog'm hon,* the Creator is asked to
protect the salmon and replenish them. Also, one asks the creator to protect
the fishermen as they fish on the river. Above all, one asks forgiveness from
the Creator for having to destroy creatures smaller than oneself in order to
sustain one's life.

In terms of keeping track of *wilp* obligations, especially when it comes to
burials or the passing and succession of a *Sigidim haanak'a,* the current or incoming *Sigidim haanak'a* is responsible for managing *wilp* resources in order
that all members can contribute to the *yukw* of others or a *li'ligit* hosted by
the *wilp.* This entails knowing what surplus food and cash is available from
each household, so that the *wilp* can sponsor or contribute substantively to
any one of the *li'ligits* the *wilp* has been invited to. Furthermore, it is the responsibility of the *Sigidim haanak'a* to pay particular attention to the ritual
aspects of the *li'ligit* in question, ensuring that *wilp* members are informed
and practiced in their roles for the event. The *li'ligit* is informed by a set of
laws and rituals that emphasizes the de-centralized and independent nature
of Gitxsan *huwilp,* while at the same time reiterating the principles of sharing
and reciprocity.

It is at the *yukw,* or feasts associated with funerals, especially, that the
initiation of the *Sigidim haanak'a* or *Simgigyet* can be considered the central
institution of the Gitxsan, as it is at the core of their social and landholding
system. During these series of *yukws* (which may take up to several years to
complete), the host *wilp* displays and performs the *wilp's ayuks* and may relate
the *adawaak* either as a narrative or through the presentation of a play ac-
companied by songs and dances. It is at these *yukws* that the relationship between the *huwilp* and the *lax'wiiyip* is brought to life. Gifts of food and other
items are first announced and then served to those present. It is at the *yukw,*
through the public display of *ayuks* and the telling of the *adawaak* witnessed
by other *Sigidim haanak'a* from one's own *wil'na t'ahl, wilksiwitxw,* and other
pteexs, that the hosting *wilp* and the *Sigidim haanak'a* validate and affirm her
claim of ownership to the *lax'wiiyip.*

It is at a *yukw* that the Gitxsan formalize their social, political, and legal
affairs. Acquisitions and inheritance of *wams* and *lax'wiiyip,* declarations of
rights of access, marriage agreements, and trade alliances are all validated and
witnessed at these *yukws.* It is at the *yukw* that the *dax gyet* — the power of
life in all creatures and in the land itself — is displayed. This is expressed and
acknowledged through the acting out of the *nax nox* of the *wilp.* The *dax gyet*

is expressed as a showing of wealth that comes from the ability to manage the *wilp's* resources on the *lax'wiiyip* for the well-being of all members. *Ax Gwin Desxw* called this the "feast economy," and testified at trial:

> At the *yukw* there is a redistribution of the wealth. Certain individuals, like people from your father's side, are commissioned to undertake certain tasks, and whatever wealth you have is transferred or given over to these people. Whatever money or gifts you have taken in, is given back.
>
> At the end of the *yukw*, money is given out to the high ranking chiefs, to your father's side or whomever you have asked to do certain things for the main house group.
>
> Also the food you bring to the feast is given out to all the other guests in the feast hall. There is usually more than enough food and some is given out at the end of the *yukw*, it is redistributed. This is called *ligii will*, and it means all the gifts and all the food in your possession represents the wealth of a particular house. The more food you have indicates the wealth of that particular chief in that house group.
>
> We always used to live off the land. All the food and all the activity came from the land, and you ensured that you prepared berries, you prepared moose meat, bear meat, salmon, you did all these things, and planned out the amount of food that you have to survive all winter, and to give at a *yukw*.
>
> They can distribute other things if they want. I have seen where they have distributed guns that are worth a thousand dollars, and TVs. I can see that in the future when we have the rightful economic benefits from our territories that we could give more valuable things as we gain the economic benefit from our territories and redistribute this in the feast system.[80]

During the performance of the *nax nox*, or if the *nax nox* touches the guests, those performing or touched are compensated. *Nax nox* is either owned by the *wilp* or by individuals. This power is acquired by an event or events experienced on the *lax'wiiyip*. In historic times, the *Sigidim haanak'as* or *Simgigyets* would be given a feather or eagle down. Now, as *Gyoluugyat* explained, they are given money:

> If the chiefs at the *yukw* have been touched by this *Nax nox*, or a song, you give them money. Before money we gave each a feather or down.

The feather or down would be given after the *nax nox* went around. The host chief now gives money out and records the name of the chief who has been given money, because this money has to be returned during another feasting.

The same way with *nax nox*, and there is a time at the feasting that a chief would make a dance, a song is sung, a person is in their regalia and this is what we call *Gus maga 'mix kaax*. This is the "returning of the down or the feather."[81]

According to Richard Daly, at the root of Gitxsan ownership is the management of the labour to access their resources, and this is expressed at any one of the Gitxsan *li'ligit*:

The nature of the relationship between proprietor and land is one of balanced, reciprocal interaction, not at all unlike that which carries on between two founding clans in a village, or between two Houses in a mother's side-father's side relationship to one another. The land is the material foundation of the House, the basis for the very social identity and history of its members.[82]

These inter-House relations that deal with both use and the proprietorship of territory, and use and proprietorship of kinship labour and fertility are symbolized by the payments that go on in the feast hall. Announcements about family business, and the accompanying exchange of gifts and services between the sides of the family work to legitimize relationships which each child has with the House of both parents. These Houses acknowledge the rights of the children, through their whole lifetime, to use and enjoy the benefits from the land and labour of the two Houses with which they are most intimately connected. These relations between Houses are in essence economic even though they have vivid domestic, political and legal dimensions as well.[83]

Gitxsan tenure and ownership arise, and are maintained, through the fulfillment of obligations to others, in combination with title to the land itself. Gitxsan society is predicated on the acknowledgement that, in the distant past, disputes have arisen, and that the sanctity of life, both human and animal, warrants respect. Since the return to the *lax'wiiyip* after the fall of *T'am Lax amit*, the Gitxsan have adhered to the *ayooks* of the hunt and fishery, and against trespass onto another's *lax'wiiyip*, as recorded in individual *wilp* and *huwilp adawaaks*. *Wilp* members look to the *Sigidim haanak'a* or *Simgigyet* to manage *wilp* resources in order that individual *wilp* members can support their families, and the *dax gyet* of the *wilp* is contingent on the *wilp* being able to fulfill its ritual obligations.

Regardless of how the *Sigidim haanak'a* or *Simgigyet* is chosen, she must be endorsed by other *Sigidim haanak'a* and *Simgigyet* at a *yukw*. The individual must have the necessary character to be able to fulfill the responsibilities, duties, and obligations that come with the office. Gitxsan governance starts when the individual is given a *wa'ayin wam*, or a name that permits one to enter and witness the events at a *yukw*, conferring the right to witness community leadership decisions. After one is able to sit at a *yukw*, one has the potential to become the *Sigidim haanak'a*, a lifelong station. The chosen one must be capable of holding the office, fulfill the ceremonial duties, and manage the *lax'wiiyip* for the benefit of *wilp* members. If the current *Sigidim haanak'a* is a woman, her brother is usually chosen to look after the *lax'wiiyip* and manage the fishery, hunting, and trapping. If the *Simgigyet* is a man, he would make most of the final decisions with respect to the *lax'wiiyip* in consultation with other *wilp* members, and he would delegate responsibilities according to the strengths of the individuals in the *wilp*.

It is at the *yukw* that the allocation of access rights is confirmed and announced to the community, as well as an accounting of *wilp* resources that have come from the *lax'wiiyip*. It is also at a *yukw* that the social and political relationships among the Gitxsan are illustrated and affirmed. When *Sigidim haanak'a* and *Simgigyet* from the *huwilp*, in turn, recount their *adawaak* and perform their *nax nox*, they are illustrating their relationship, both historic and current.

An additional role of the *Sigidim haanak'a* is to settle disputes and provide leadership for the community. Disputes that arise within the *wilp* are usually settled within the *wilp*. However, if settlement is not possible, other *Sigidim haanak'a* and *Simgigyet* are called in, according to the tradition of *sisixsek*. Likewise, when there is a larger problem that affects the entire community, it is the *Sigidim haanak'a* and *Simgigyet*, in consultation with *wilp* members, who are called on to make the necessary decisions. The *Sigidim haanak'a* and *Simgigyet* will listen to *wilp* members, and eventually they will intervene and give direction to form a consensus. Consensus building requires that the *Sigidim haanak'a* and *Simgigyet* be well informed on the issue, either consulting with *wilp* members or leading the debate.

All Gitxsan are taught the *adawaaks* from their father's and mother's families. It is in the *adawaak* that the boundaries of individual *lax'wiiyip* have been recorded, and reference is made to the *ayuks*. *Ayuks* may be either exclusive to a *wilp* or shared by a series of *wilps*. The *adawaaks*, in narrative form, also hold the important *ayooks* of the *wilp* that govern how the Gitxsan people must behave toward one another, as well as while fishing, hunting, and gathering food, and how the *Sigidim haanak'a* and *Simgigyet* must perform management tasks and dispute resolution duties. Property relations, for the Gitxsan, are maintained by strict adherence to the *ayooks*, as spoken in the *adawaaks*, which are premised on respect and recognition.

Since the coming of the *Lixs giigyet* and the establishment of the reserve system, the Crown has afforded little acknowledgement, understanding, or accommodation to Gitxsan laws, land tenure, or management schemes in either federal or provincial law. The ability of the Gitxsan to adhere to their boundaries and act within their *ayooks* has been severely compromised.

CHAPTER FIVE

Gitxsan Reconciliation

THROUGH PETITIONS, STATEMENTS, AND DELEGATIONS, THE GITXSAN HAVE sought a means of embedding their *ayooks* and customs into the fabric of Canada. In 1984 they filed suit against the province as a means of compelling a negotiated settlement situated in their laws. They anticipated that, by presenting *ayooks* as a basis of their governance, resource management, and ownership of their territories, the courts could see that they had remained faithful to their traditions, and desired to maintain their traditional governance structure in conjunction with provincial ministries.

As a result of their litigation,[1] following the challenges of other British Columbia First Nations,[2] the courts encouraged all parties to negotiate settlements through the existing treaty process. If the community elects to litigate their claim of title or rights, the Supreme Court has created a test for Aboriginal rights and has delineated the parameters and content of Aboriginal title. It has encouraged the Crown to reconcile with First Nations and added consultation and compensation for infringement of their rights and title to the list of existing fiduciary obligations of the Crown. Currently, the Gitxsan have only negotiated an Interim Forest Agreement in the Kispiox watershed (October 24, 2006) and have yet to come to an agreement as to the shape of their relationship with the Crown in Right of Canada and British Columbia. The Land Question for the Gitxsan remains unfinished business.

The federal government stated its position on comprehensive claims in August 1973, and subsequent policy in 1981 stipulated that the community's Aboriginal title was to be ceded in exchange for a modified title (entitlement lands), user rights within the traditional territory, and a compensation package.[3] In the latest comprehensive claims development, as set out in the 1993 Liberal Party platform document, "The Aboriginal Peoples of Canada," there is no required blanket extinguishment of Aboriginal rights in exchange for modified rights and title; however, First Nations are required to provide certainty with respect to land rights, and finality regarding compensation. Currently, the British Columbia and federal governments are negotiating agreements that fall within these parameters with respect to land rights and compensation,[4] and are using a model of self-government that has a combination of municipal and provincial-like powers, limited to a specified land base.[5]

In essence, First Nations communities are being granted an enlarged reserve, defined in terms of fee simple, that will permit them to leverage outside investment without surrendering their territorial base, that will recognize their rights of ownership and management of resources on those lands (trees and minerals, but not oil and gas), and hold modified Aboriginal rights, subject to other First Nations and newcomer interests, throughout their traditional territories. The community, whether negotiating as a tribal council or an individual community, is expected to settle any overlap amongst themselves in keeping with the constitutional principle that the affairs of the First Nation are not matters for the Crown.

Past Usage of the Crown

In the past, the Crown, drawing on the principles of the *Royal Proclamation of 1763*, has negotiated with First Nations to work out the terms of surrender and their continued rights on Crown lands. Generally, at the onset of treaty discussions, Crown representatives have acknowledged the community's traditional territory and land use, and have set aside a fixed acreage as a reserve for their exclusive use and benefit within the territory. Resources such as timber and mining leases on reserve lands have been negotiated for sale or lease by government, subject to the approval of the community, and the sales, lease, or royalties set aside for the benefit of the community. When the Crown required additional lands for roads, waterways, railroads, public works, and settlements, it purchased the reserve lands outright, leased them, or provided the community with alternate lands. The First Nations' interest in the land at the time of surrender, however, was deemed to be less than fee simple, and contingent on the prevailing attitude toward First Nations' rights. In general, Aboriginal and treaty rights have been limited to hunting, fishing, and trapping, and to ceremonial and social use. In some instances, communities have pressed for additional activities to be deemed rights, having shown that they are specific activities that make them distinctive.[6]

Along this road of reconciliation, there have been attempts by both the federal government and First Nations to rectify the situation. During the debates following the 1969 White Paper on Indian policy,[7] it was apparent that First Nations across Canada sought a renewed relationship with the federal government that would enable them to settle grievances that were either situated in the treaty relationship or related to the cut-off lands the McKenna-McBride Commission created. At the same time, the federal cabinet sought to transfer First Nations' responsibilities to the provinces. The White Paper also put forward a proposition that would see reserve lands, existing trusts and annuities divided equally among band members.

Where treaties had been signed, it appeared that the "cede and surrender" agreements the communities had entered into in exchange for protection were being disregarded. Although the government wanted to divest itself of "Indians and Indian lands," it was willing to act on its lawful obligations when it came to past grievances regarding the sale or lease of reserve lands or fraud with respect to the acquisition or dispossession of reserve lands by employees or agents of the federal government. In British Columbia, the federal government was willing to examine the rationale and results related to the cut-off lands that had been taken as a result of the findings of the McKenna-McBride Commission. With respect to First Nations communities that had not entered into agreements of surrender, the government argued that Aboriginal title claims were too general to be capable of specific remedy. Needless to say, the White Paper was shelved, and little was accomplished until the Nisga'a took their claim to the Supreme Court in November 1971.

In the *Calder* case, the Nisga'a sought to establish that their Aboriginal title in the Nass Valley had not been extinguished prior to British Columbia's entrance into Confederation in 1871.[8] Although the Supreme Court's ruling, rendered in January 1973, was inconclusive, the *Calder* decision made it clear that Aboriginal title was alive as a legal concept and prompted the Trudeau government to revise its stance with respect to First Nations that had yet to enter into formal surrender agreements with the Crown. The year the Nisga'a went to the Supreme Court, 16 chiefs filed a *caveat* on the title to approximately 700,000 square kilometres in the Northwest Territories, based on the claim that they had never ceded their Aboriginal rights.[9] The James Bay Cree, that year, in a similar argument, obtained an injunction to halt the construction of a hydro-electric dam at James Bay.[10] After the success of *Calder* and these other First Nations actions, the federal government modified its position and has attempted, over the years, to settle these outstanding concerns. The legal grounds for Aboriginal title claims were expanded in 1984 with the *Guerin* decision, which provided a judicial remedy to First Nations for breach of the fiduciary obligations owed to them by the Crown.[11] In 1990, the fiduciary obligations of the Crown were raised to the constitutional level when the Supreme Court ruled in *Sparrow* that "existing aboriginal and treaty rights of the aboriginal peoples of Canada were hereby recognized and affirmed."[12]

Although the federal government has, since 1973, been willing to discuss Aboriginal rights in broad terms and, to a large degree, hand over defined land and management rights, it has insisted on the co-operation of the provincial or territorial government concerned in fulfilling treaty obligations or concluding title claims. In 1973, the federal Comprehensive Claims Policy could arguably be characterized in terms of the past usage of the Crown, meaning that the community had to agree to the prerequisite of blanket extinguishment in exchange for conferred rights. In their 1975 treaty,[13] for example, the James Bay Cree, having agreed to cede and surrender their traditional lands, received lands partitioned into three categories. On Category I lands, the Cree hold title exclusively, and these lands can only be surrendered to the Province of Quebec. The Province of Quebec owns the mineral and subsurface rights, but their dispensation is administered according to *Indian Act* standards, so if Quebec requires access to these resources, other lands or compensation will be offered in exchange. Category II lands are under provincial control; however, any mineral extraction is subject to the consent of the community, and Cree and Inuit Aboriginal user rights must be accommodated. If Quebec requires land for the purpose of development, the land will either be replaced or compensation will be awarded. Category III grants to all persons, First Nation and Newcomers alike, access to subsistence resources under provincial laws, but only First Nations people have year-round access for hunting, fishing, trapping, and cutting wood without a permit. In terms of governance, the entire region operates under the jurisdiction of the Municipality of James Bay, where local communities are able to pass by-laws, subject to veto by the municipality. The James Bay Treaty is similar to the numbered treaties in that the James Bay Cree have a demarcated land base. Unlike the numbered treaties, however, the ownership of resources on reserves is vested in the Province of Quebec — though some benefit returns to the community — and the James Bay Cree have Aboriginal rights use, subject to regulation by Quebec, throughout their traditional territory.

In separate negotiations that started in the wake of the James Bay agreement and the Berger Inquiry into the proposed Mackenzie River pipeline,[14] the Inuvialuit at the mouth of the Mackenzie River concluded the Inuvialuit Final Agreement in 1984.[15] It is not unlike the James Bay agreement in that the community ceded and surrendered its territory in exchange for set rights, but it organizes the reserve in a slightly different fashion. The Inuvialuit structured their reserve lands and governance along a traditional conception of their rights and the differences between themselves and their southern indigenous neighbours. They sought to protect the lands they moved across in pursuit of caribou, their inland fisheries, and access to the shoreline in order to reach marine mammals and fish.

The thrust of the Inuvialuit agreement is for the protection of wildlife and traditional pursuits while permitting eco-friendly development. Their subsequent institutions, such as the Land Use Planning Commission and the Land Use Applications and Review Committee, are intrinsic to the regulation of these non-industrial activities. Controlled by the Inuit, their purpose is to assist the territorial governments — at that time only the Yukon and Northwest Territories — with the administration of land use regulations, as well as to develop systems and procedures for administering environmental standards in the region.

The Nunavut Agreement of 1993 took what was initiated by the Inuvialuit a step further.[16] First, the Tungavik Federation of Nunavut, like the Inuvialuit, own in fee simple approximately 18 per cent of the land (accepted as Inuit entitlement lands), and on that land they own 10 per cent of the subsurface rights. As in the Western Arctic Agreement, the Tungavik Inuit have various boards overseeing the management of these lands in conjunction with the territorial government of Nunavut. Although the Inuit make up 80 per cent of the population and are in essence self-governing, the remaining 82 per cent of the land is defined as federal Crown lands, and Nunavut, as a territory, does not hold title either to the lands or the non-renewable resources; nor does it exercise exclusive legislative authority. Although currently a territory, Nunavut anticipates provincial status, following which the dominance of Ottawa to be replaced by local administrative structures composed mainly of Inuit. For the time being, Nunavut lands and resources are co-managed between Ottawa and Nunavut. The Nunavut Wildlife Management Board, the Nunavut Impact Review Board, the Nunavut Planning Commission, the Surface Rights Tribunal, and the Nunavut Water Board are to work with Ottawa to ensure that Inuit rights are maintained in conjunction with regional development.

Despite the *Calder* decision of 1973, it was not until 1990 that the Province of British Columbia agreed to negotiate a settlement with the Nisga'a and the federal government. Currently, the Nisga'a have the only modern treaty with both the federal and provincial governments in British Columbia. Their treaty sought to encapsulate and acknowledge their continued struggle since 1884 to reach an equitable solution to their land question, and pressed for recognition of their Aboriginal title based on their historic use and occupation of the Nass Valley. Canada and British Columbia were able to embrace the Nisga'a goal of a contiguous land base that encompassed their core territories, the Oolichan spawning grounds, and a majority of their salmon fishing sites, a process that put the administration of their affairs outside the *Indian Act* and created a model of self-government that went beyond village administration.

The Nisga'a felt they could accommodate the Crown's requirement that they pay personal and corporate income taxes if they were to bring economic development into the Nass that would be reflected in the lives of the Nisga'a people. The Nisga'a elected to negotiate their fishing rights in a separate agreement — the Harvest Agreement — that does not guarantee a specific quota but ensures that, whatever quota is allocated to them, they will have complete say as to its use. That is, the Nisga'a can reassign numbers relative to overall salmon returns, and they have the freedom to sell, process, or consume the fish themselves. In order to achieve the contiguous land base they desired and the construction and maintenance of paved roads within and linking their communities, the Nisga'a agreed to the development of *Anhluult'ukwsim Laxmihl Angwinga'asan Nisga'a*, the Nisga'a Memorial Lava Bed Provincial Park, and relinquished title to the land beneath the roads to the province.

Pursuant to the federal government's comprehensive claims policy, treaty negotiations commenced in 1976 with the Discussion Paper on Indian Land Claims in BC[17] based on Jean Chrétien's 1973 commitment as Minister of Indian Affairs and Northern Development.[18] Despite the shift in federal policy with respect to resolving claims by First Nations where there were no formal surrenders, British Columbia elected to participate only as an observer. It was not until 1990 that the province became a full participant. When the BC Minister for Native Affairs, Jack Weisgerber, signed a framework agreement with the federal Minister of Indian Affairs and Northern Development, Tom Siddon, and Nisga'a Tribal Council President Alvin McKay and six other Nisga'a leaders, it was the first indication that the Aboriginal title question in British Columbia could be resolved.[19]

The Nisga'a Final Agreement rests on the premise of certainty in exchange for definitions to inherent as well as delegated rights.[20] It provides for a constitution, outlines Nisga'a villages and the Nisga'a *Lisims* government, and has a separate fishing agreement. The Nisga'a have been granted, in fee simple, a 2,000-square-kilometre land base along the Nass (in Nisga'a, *Lisims*) River for their exclusive use and occupation. Nisga'a-designated lands outside this area are partitioned into various categories of exclusivity, which reflect Nisga'a traditional use and the need for the people to be engaged in the regional economy. It also enables the provincial government to accommodate Nisga'a site-specific Aboriginal rights. In the separate Harvest Agreement, and not constitutionally protected, the Nisga'a have access to Nass River salmon and the oolichan fishery in proportion to the estimated run, limited by conservation and use by other stakeholders. Only on Nisga'a lands do the Nisga'a people, under a Constitution outlining the powers of their government, have the capacity to make laws, in keeping with federal and provincial standards, with respect to land use, language, and culture. Outside Nisga'a lands, the Nisga'a have been given both Aboriginal user rights and first refusal of any forest tenure to the extent of their traditional boundaries. The Nisga'a Nation has been given a priority right to back-country tenures or agricultural leases for the purpose of economic development. In these lands, the provincial government and the Nisga'a Nation expect to co-manage the tenures, especially with respect to forestry licenses and mining leases, subject to any overlapping claim by other First Nations in the region. Although in these peripheral lands the provincial government holds exclusive jurisdiction, it acknowledges Aboriginal user rights for fishing, hunting, trapping, and the gathering of foodstuffs; some Nisga'a rights are contingent on neighbouring First Nations' rights of exclusivity or first refusal. If the government requires lands in these areas that put Nisga'a rights in jeopardy, the Nisga'a expect to be consulted, and will be compensated accordingly, either by an exchange of land or through a cash settlement. Both the provincial and federal governments have received certainty with respect to land rights, and have accepted responsibility for the costs of the post-treaty relationship.

In order to meet the Crown as equals and to speak with one voice, the Nisga'a elected in 1890 to place their lands in a "common bowl" and, as early as 1888, had administrative control over their village affairs. Nisga'a *Simigat* (male hereditary chiefs) and *Sigidimhaanak* (matriarchs) modified their *ayuuks* of governance to accommodate the newcomers' concept of democracy, as laid out in the *Indian Act, 1884,* choosing to elect their village leaders in accordance with prevailing standards. Although they hold elections, the community agreed that only *Simigat* were eligible to run for band council office. This, they said, was to preserve continuity between Nisga'a law and the expectations of the newcomers. The decision to go forward in 1888 with band councils according to the *Indian Advancement Act,* 1884,[21] was reached by consensus under the urging of Anglican missionaries.[22]

The Nisga'a have accepted the terms of a delegated municipal-style government, with some provincial-like powers limited to Nisga'a Lands and over Nisga'a citizens. The Nisga'a Constitution formalizes the authority of the village governments and the central Nisga'a *Lisims* Government over their election practices, assets, and forms of marriage; it supports Nisga'a language and cultural values, and accepts the Canadian *Criminal Code* and the *Charter of Rights and Freedoms.* More specifically, it provides for the creation of Nisga'a Urban Locals for Nisga'a citizens who reside outside the Nass Valley, allowing them to participate in Nisga'a *Lisims* Government. In addition to the powers of their government, the Constitution makes provisions for Nisga'a elders to interpret the *ayuuks* to the Nisga'a *Lisims* Government. Where there is a conflict, Nisga'a jurisdiction and legislative authority on Nisga'a lands and over Nisga'a citizens will prevail over federal or provincial laws. Outside Nisga'a lands, however, Nisga'a *ayuuks* will not have any effect, and disputes between British Columbia and the Nisga'a will be resolved according to provincial policy. All these provisions are defined in detail in the Nisga'a Final Agreement, which came into effect on May 11, 2000.

What the Nisga'a achieved is distinctly different from the goals of the Gitxsan. Although the federal Crown no longer uses the terms that require First Nations to cede and surrender their lands in exchange for an exhaustive list of rights, it still insists on a demarcated land base, and will not re-open the terms of treaty after the agreement has been passed into legislation. Furthermore, the federal treaty mandate with British Columbia First Nations is couched in terms of the 1993 Memorandum of Understanding between the provincial and federal governments: contemporary treaties in British Columbia are seen as the beginning of a process that shifts administrative responsibilities for First Nations from the Department of Indian Affairs and Northern Development onto the provincial government and the First Nations community. As Federal Minister of Indian and Northern Affairs Ron Irwin pointed out, treaty settlements are perceived as down payments for "the provincialization of aboriginal services."[23]

The province, like the federal government, seeks a clear definition of territorial and Aboriginal user rights, and wants assurance that First Nations will relinquish their tax-free status, integrate their land use plans on their enlarged reserves, and, in the peripheral lands, demark Aboriginal user rights locations and harmonize these practices with provincial fiscal concerns and regulatory practices.[24] Although the federal government acknowledges, as policy, First Nations' inherent right to self-government, it insists that final jurisdiction over the community must be negotiated with the province (and in some cases municipalities) to determine the extent of First Nations' legislative powers.

Similarly, the provincial Crown's idea of reconciliation is based on a tiered relationship with the land, access to specific resources, and more clearly defined areas where community members may exercise their Aboriginal rights. The province is willing to add up to 20 per cent more territory to existing reserves for the community's exclusive use and occupation.[25] On vacant Crown lands outside fee simple lands, First Nations will be asked to identify locations where Aboriginal rights' activities will likely be undertaken, which will then be set aside for their use, subject to Crown consultation and regulation. A third category of land use gives the First Nation community access to their Aboriginal rights use that is similar to general vacant Crown land; however, the First Nation in question would be restrained by other First Nation use of this territory. The First Nations community will have broader rights to particular resources on these enlarged reserves, and, where appropriate, the community will be given the right of first refusal on agricultural, grazing, or mining leases, and will be eligible to bid on government contracts and forest tenure licenses within their traditional territories. Through the identification of locations where Aboriginal rights activities could occur on vacant Crown lands, the province feels confident that it can meet its fiduciary obligations of consultation[26] and, if necessary, accommodation and compensation through its October 2002 "Provincial Policy for Consultation with First Nations."

Self-government is limited to settlement lands as stipulated by the treaty, and First Nations' ability to make law is limited to municipal affairs, language, culture, and land use within its borders. Governance will be negotiated outside the final agreement and will not be constitutionally protected under Sections 25 or 35 of the *Constitution Act, 1982*. First Nations government structures are to be determined by a constitution, be democratically elected, fiscally accountable, and adhere to standards generally accepted by other Canadian governments. Finally, the federal government has agreed to pay compensation to the community based on a ratio determined by the cost of additional lands and resources transferred to the community from the province, minus the costs of negotiations.[27] Additional funds will be allocated to the community to assist with treaty implementation, and support for self-government is to be shared between the federal and provincial governments.[28] The current model for self government does not allow the community to greatly influence land use throughout their traditional territories outside their treaty settlement lands, except through a consultation process that will be limited to access to Section 35 rights once the ink is dry.

Gitxsan Acts of Reconciliation

The Supreme Court of Canada in 1997 set out an expanded definition of Aboriginal title, its proof, and the inherent limit of such title. It also stated the conditions under which governments might infringe upon it. The court also granted the Gitxsan the opportunity for a re-trial based on the belief that, if the trial judge had given the oral history its rightful significance, the conclusion of the trial would have been different. Like the Nisga'a, the Gitxsan put forward their claim to territory and their historic vision of reconciliation of their ownership with the Crown's sovereignty. However, their vision of the reconciled relationship is distinctly different from that of the Nisga'a. The Gitxsan hold and use their *lax'wiiyip* as *wilp* members, coming together as a community to make decisions as allied *wilps*, or the *Gim litxwid*[29] respecting the office of the *Sigidim haanak'a* or *Simgigyet*.

The Gitxsan, after the 1997 decision, offered both the federal and provincial governments a means to re-start the treaty-making negotiations suspended in February 1995. In their Reconciliation Agreement,[30] the Gitxsan proposed that the talks be premised on the principles of *amnigwootxw* and *xkyeehl,* that draw on the *dax gyet* of the *Sigidim haanak'as* or *Simgigyets* to make penultimate decisions about the disposition and allocation of *wilp* resources. Specifically, they desired to enter into a formal relationship with Canada that would permit Canada continual and full access to their entire *lax'wiiyip* in exchange for meaningful protection of their Aboriginal user rights, and they envisioned that their association with the province would be more of a business relationship.

Accordingly, the Gitxsan's connection with Canada would be situated on the principles of *amnigwootxw,* or permission for one outside the *wilp* to use their territory and resources in exchange for good deeds done. They envisioned that topics discussed between themselves and Canada at the treaty table would revolve around consultation protocols that would ensure that Canada's agencies and departments, as well as the provincial government, adhere to a set of conditions for the protection of their Aboriginal rights when either Crown proposed to use the land or allocate a resource to third parties. This would necessitate that Canada trust the Gitxsan to be active managers of their Aboriginal rights, and understand the primary responsibility the Gitxsan have to the land, the fish, the animals, and the plants. The Gitxsan have always understood that the land itself must be groomed to remain productive, so activities such as forestry, agriculture, mining, roads, and settlements have their place — but not at the expense of the animals, the plants, the fish, the land itself, or the Gitxsan's ability to access them for food, ceremony, or social purposes. The Gitxsan feel that the Gitxsan-Canada relationship should be based on privileged reciprocity,[31] in that Canada must find a means to protect Gitxsan interests that does not erode their Section 35 (1) rights, or lessen their capability to control their Section 35 (1) use, in light of other legitimate uses of their territory by the Crown.[32] This suggests that language, culture, and related education interests are of primary importance to the Gitxsan, and should be of federal concern. It is also important that Canada support the Gitxsan in their relationship with the provincial Crown when legislative interference is inevitable.

At this time, the principle of *xkyeehl* would be initiated between the Gitxsan and British Columbia, permitting the former to negotiate protection of their known Aboriginal rights and engage in a consultation process that could place community economic needs inside the project, or to negotiate appropriate compensation.[33] Compensation tables could be negotiated for industries, transportation corridors, and other items in general, with room for periodic review and a dispute-resolution process. This model assumes that all Gitxsan territory is used for the pursuit of Aboriginal rights and that all territory could be classified as Aboriginal title; as such, the provincial Crown would be obligated to discuss with the Gitxsan its alternate use, and its assessment of compensation for justifiable infringement.

The Gitxsan could formally cede to the federal Crown its land, with protective clauses outlining the terms of how the federal government would protect Gitxsan Aboriginal rights, given provincial land use plans with respect to forestry, recreation, mineral exploitation, wildlife management, and transportation for all newcomers. With respect to Gitxsan and provincial Crown renewed relations, the Gitxsan expect to work out a more tempered, business-like relationship based on *xkyeehl,* which would allow British Columbia access to their *lax'wiiyip.* In this way, consultation protocols are stressed, and decision-making regarding territorial use, as well as compensation for the access and use of non-Aboriginal rights resources on and in the *lax'wiiyip,* is expected. The establishment of a business-like relationship could assist in rectifying the historical position of the provincial Crown toward First Nations' territories in light of its previous position of unilateral extinguishment of their Aboriginal rights with respect to land.

In terms of Gitxsan culture, when it comes to the sharing of resources from the *lax'wiiyip*, the *wilp* not only has a proprietary interest in the specific resources that come directly from their holdings, they can call on family — cousins or relatives by marriage — to assist them in maximizing their access to these resources, especially fishing, berry picking, and the mountain goat hunt. The *wilp*, by accepting the labour of others, assumes the obligation of sharing the resources among them according to their participation, their status in the *wilp*, and the need for the *wilp* to "put aside" for its social obligations. *Wilp* economy depends not only on *huwilp* connections by *yuugwilatxw* (marriage), *pteex* affiliations, political alliances, or obligations created by *amnigwootxw, xkyeehl,* or by *xsiisx*, but also relies on the social ties that any Gitxsan may bring to his or her *wilp* with different resources throughout the territory claimed by the Gitxsan. Those outside the *wilp*, by accepting access to specific resources through the principles of *amnigwootxw*, also accept the obligation to assist the *wilp* at ceremonial events through resource contributions, mainly at funerals or during the pole-raising feasts. Similarly, when a *wilp* accepts *xkyeehl*, it is obligated to accommodate those who have asked for access to *wilp* resources. It is within this internal economic system of reciprocity that the Gitxsan believe they may establish a nation-to-nation relationship with Canada and a working/managerial relationship with British Columbia.

The concepts of *amnigwootxw* and *xkyeehl* establish a means for the Gitxsan and the state — both Canada and British Columbia — to interact with the land and the resources on it in terms of a hierarchy of interests. For example, with land and resources, a series of interests can be readily built up, as property in land and resources is characteristically distributed as a series of rights that can be held by different segments of society, and at times simultaneously. Thus, the Gitxsan can divest themselves of exclusivity through extending *amnigwootxw* privileges to Canada in exchange for protection for their Aboriginal rights activities. This type of relationship could be read as a form of cede and surrender, but if Canada failed to protect Aboriginal interests as defined by treaty, the Gitxsan would be guaranteed certainty and have the means of redress and compensation.

Similarly, the Gitxsan-British Columbia relationship, if built on the principles of *xkyeehl*, would enable the Gitxsan and the province to establish compensation indices that would reflect existing infringements and future resource development on a case-by-case basis. Thus, the cost of the British Columbia-Gitxsan relationship would be dependent on what percentage of Gitxsan territory would be annexed for development, the degree of disturbance, and the time period. On the pragmatic level, the Gitxsan want to move the debate out of the certainty and finality policy toward a model that speaks to their rights of access to resources throughout the entire *wilp lax'wiiyip*, their obligations and duties to each other, and their historic and continued relationship with the land itself.

The Gitxsan Treaty Model

The starting point for the Gitxsan treaty model is that Gitxsan interests encompass fish, game, and fur. Since their main objectives are to prevent and circumvent damage to their *lax'wiiyip,* and as they have co-existed with the salmon and other wildlife for thousands of years and wish to continue to do so, they would rather avoid being paid compensation for this loss. The Gitxsan are not simply passive consumers of these resources; they have managed them in order that they are there to be harvested. Further, the relationship the Gitxsan have with their *lax'wiiyip* is inseparable from their identity. They are who they are because of their relationship with the land. Although they no longer rely entirely on hunting, fishing, and trapping for their subsistence, and are engaged in the *Lixs giigyet* economy, this does not refute who they are or their obligations to the *lax'wiiyip.*

The Gitxsan believe that Canada, British Columbia, and the *Simgigyet* or *Sigidim haanak'a* collectively need to set protocols for co-management and consultation in order that the Gitxsan will be apprised of any legislative initiative leading to infringement by either British Columbia or Canada that affects their ability to access their known Aboriginal rights on their territory with respect to fish, animals, berries, and fowl, so that they can meaningfully participate in discussions that will lead to appropriate solutions for infringement or compensation. As for the ability to regulate environmental standards, they hope that Canada will continue to assist them with education and training, according to their Reconciliation Agreement, to enable them to achieve the necessary standings with respect to enforcement and remain competitive with the newcomers for alternative employment in the region.

The Gitxsan believe they are in the best position to manage the wildlife that resides in and passes through their territories, and expect Canada to support them in this matter. They believe, at minimum, that they have the Aboriginal right to hunt, trap, gather, and fish in the lands they have occupied since time immemorial. As they feel that there are going to be legitimate provincial infringements onto their Aboriginal user rights, they are prepared to work out the terms and the consultative protocols with British Columbia.[34] However, in keeping with the principles of *xkyeehl*, payment should be allocated, both formalizing the commitment to allow British Columbia use of the *lax'wiiyip* and ensuring that the Gitxsan are compensated for the loss of rights to their traditional livelihood in the region.

Fish, Wildlife, and Fur

The Gitxsan understand that salmon and other animals know no boundaries, so an enlarged land base through claims negotiations does not guarantee that their needs will continue to be met, nor does it ensure that the lands necessary for the existence of the animals or fish will remain immune from third party damage or alternate use. They have therefore maintained that they should be actively engaged in the regulation of the fishery and habitat.[35]

Regarding fish and other Section 35 resources, the Gitxsan feel they can provide Canada with the locations of *wilp* fishing sites and habitat ranges for specific animals, as well as provide detailed information on the number of salmon and other species captured, as it is in the best interests of all parties. In terms of the seasonal management of the salmon fishery, the Gitxsan believe that the minimum allocation should reflect their consumption requirements and fulfill their trade obligations. Moreover, they wish to maintain their Section 35 fishing rights, be allocated a commercial inland river fishery, and receive funding to support habitat restoration. They believe they can work with the Department of Fisheries and Oceans supporting the current direction in management and policy development that established regional consultative bodies. The Aboriginal Aquatic Resource and Ocean Management Program (AAROM) approaches the allocation of fish and aquatic resources from the perspective that First Nations can play a large and significant role in the management of fisheries resources.[36] The Gitxsan feel they must be able to participate in the collection of information as well as with the operational aspects of fisheries management. As this initiative encompasses all users, including the sports inland fishery, which is under provincial jurisdiction, the Gitxsan are confident that this level of co-operation will assist in maintaining their allocation numbers, as well as sustain funding for fish habitat and stream restoration. They are confident that regional management, involving representatives from all parties, will enable each *wilp* to conduct its fishery accordingly.

The Gitxsan desire full authority to assign and monitor trap lines through a Blanket Trap Line License that would encompass their entire *lax'wiiyip*.[37] More importantly, such a license would enable the *huwilp* to reclaim the right to assign trap lines within their *wilp lax'wiiyip* boundaries to *wilp* members and on the death of the *Simgigyet* or *Sigidim haanak'a*. Currently, under provincial law, trap line licenses are regulated under the Wildlife Act Commercial Activities Regulation, which covers areas related to harvest numbers and accountability. Under provincial standards, these licenses are considered private property, and on the death of the licensee, they could be transferred to anyone, Gitxsan or not. This is contrary to the notion that the territories are held by the *wilp* for *wilp* use. It is incumbent on *wilp* members to ensure that they follow the rules of harvest as set out by the *Simgigyet* or *Sigidim haanak'a*; at the death of a *Simgigyet* or *Sigidim haanak'a*, the registered trap lines would remain in possession of the *wilp*, and would subsequently be registered in the name of the *Simgigyet* or *Sigidim haanak'a*, the only authority permitted to allocate harvest numbers.

It is expected that the trapper will work according to Gitxsan *ayooks*. The *wilp* will inform the user of all trap line levies, as determined by the user's relationship to the *wilp* and set by a consensus administered by the Gitxsan Resource Management Office. The money collected will first look after administration, and second, habitat assessment and restoration. This resource directorate will be responsible for keeping track of the number of animals and the locations they were taken. Quotas for the fur harvest will be set according to prevailing Gitxsan standards, in consultation with provincial authorities. Gitxsan trappers will be encouraged to move about the territories, and if they require access to areas other than their own *wilp's lax'wiiyip*, they must seek the permission of the appropriate *Simgigyet* or *Sigidim haanak'a*. It will be up to the *Sigidim haanak'a* to authorize the resources directorate to assign access to the trapper. Those trapping in another's *lax'wiiyip* will pay an additional surcharge to the directorate, which would return to the *wilp* in question. If a *wilp* member trespasses, any traps and other equipment from the area in question will be confiscated, and fines will be levied against the trespasser.

Gitxsan *ayooks* regarding the harvesting of fish, animals, and plants are situated in their renewed contract with the animals and fish themselves: if they over-hunt, over-trap, or over-fish, the animals will not remain in their *lax'wiiyip*, the *wilp* risks not being able to sustain itself. Families share, but there is no guarantee that the *Sigidim haanak'a* or another *wilp* will extend *amnigwootxw* rights or accept *xkyeehl* if the person is known to over-exploit a resource.

Forestry

The Gitxsan's working assumptions with respect to forestry development are that disturbances to the soil and changes to the quantity or quality of stream water will in some way affect their ability to access fur, fish, and plants according to traditional use and occupation. On each *wilp lax'wiiyip*, Aboriginal rights and title are used solely by the *wilp* responsible for the specific *lax'wiiyip*, subject to Gitxsan *ayooks* and allocation decisions made by each *wilp's Sigidim haanak'a* or the person designated by her. Each *wilp* has the right, subject to Gitxsan *ayooks*, to use its fishing sites, hunting grounds, trap lines, and berry patches. The Gitxsan believe that the exercise of each *wilp's* Aboriginal rights and title requires the conservation of sufficient habitats for plants and animals on its *lax'wiiyip,* and the preservation of all cabins, camp sites, and trails. In order to achieve a balance between Aboriginal rights and title and the Crown's right to enact "compelling legislative imperatives,"[38] the Gitxsan propose that the Ministry of Forests not infringe on any *wilp's* exercise of its Aboriginal rights or title without prior consent. They also believe that the development of clear guidelines outlining conditions of infringement, and joint protocols with respect to consultation procedures can only minimize the impact of forest development on their Aboriginal rights and title.[39]

The Gitxsan believe that, in order to achieve meaningful reconciliation, consultation with the provincial Crown must reflect their ongoing Aboriginal rights and the title interests of each *wilp* before cutting permits to forest resources are allocated. They expect that the province will consult with the appropriate *wilp Simgigyet* or *Sigidim haanak'a* on a cutting plan that will not disturb the soil, change plant and animal habitat, alter the quality, quantity, or location of streams, change the means of access to the *lax'wiiyip,* or preclude future economic and educational activities by the *wilp.*[40] In such cases, it would be expected that consent will be forthcoming. Deeper consultation would be required if the ministry's proposal results in more than ten per cent of the *lax'wiiyip* area soil being disturbed.[41] In such a case, the Gitxsan would require that the ministry implement an alternative forest use proposal that achieves the same legislative objectives but does not infringe on the *wilp's* ability to exercise its Aboriginal rights and title. The consent of the *wilp* will be required if more than 10 percent but less than 30 percent of the soil is disturbed.[42] If the Ministry of Forest's proposal uses more than 30 percent of any *wilp's lax'wiiyip* at any one time, the *lax'wiiyip* will be considered unable to sustain its Aboriginal rights activity and the *wilp* will consider its ability to carry out its Aboriginal rights impossible, thus defining their *lax'wiiyip* as destroyed. At this level of infringement, the *wilp* would have the right to withhold consent.[43] If the Ministry and the Gitxsan representatives feel they are unable to reach agreement on these matters, they would follow a dispute resolution process that first seeks to resolve the matter between the Gitxsan and within the Ministry, and, as a last resort, refers the matter to a scientific panel for resolution.[44] It is expected that, as part of the relationship between Gitxsan *wilps* and the Ministry of Forests, there will be a high degree of information sharing, and that all parties entering into discussions are doing so freely and co-operatively, with the goal of finding a solution to the immediate problem.[45] The Gitxsan expect that all compensation will be directed to the *Gim litxwid* based on a negotiated agreement.

Mining, Oil, and Gas

Gitxsan concerns are focused on the long-term impact that oil and gas exploration and mining ventures will have on *wilp lax'wiiyip*, and on the revenue sharing related to the resource. Coal, copper, silver, and gold have been found on Gitxsan territories in the past, and the Gitxsan believe that any other resources would be mined according to their standards. If the potential resource exploitation were to contravene the principles of equitable waste, the Gitxsan would expect that appropriate technology be developed to accommodate resource extraction without posing an environmental hazard.

While the Supreme Court has affirmed in *Delgam'Uukw* that the First Nations community may engage in resource activities that have not been part of their historical livelihood, they may not do so to the extent that it destroys their relationship with the land. Although the Gitxsan can propose convincing arguments for oil and gas ownership based on use and occupation of the *lax'wiiyip*, they may be compelled to suspend their rights to provide the necessary security for the development of resources, including secondary industry such as the construction of sawmills. In order that the community is able to engage in seemingly contradictory Aboriginal rights and title endeavours that put their Section 35 rights or title at risk, and be able to underwrite the development of non-traditional resources, it may be necessary that the Gitxsan and Canada jointly write enabling legislation, similar to the *First Nations Commercial and Industrial Development Act* [46] for on-reserve developments, which guarantees third parties the necessary security and regulatory regimes and at the same time provides the Gitxsan with a temporary alternative definition of Aboriginal title and rights for the purposes of development.

Thus, the development goals of the Gitxsan fall into three areas: first, the assertion of their title to oil and gas and mineral resources; second, the assurance that the environmental and socio-cultural impact of energy exploration, development, transport, and use are adequately and responsibly addressed; and third, policy and procedure associated with development must ensure that future generations of Gitxsan have secure access to any benefits arising from the development of resources on the *lax'wiiyip*, and that measures are taken to ensure their efficient and conservative use. [47] Further, the federal Crown should keep to a minimum the acreage required for the development, extraction, maintenance, and delivery of oil, gas, or minerals, and environmental standards for development, extraction, and delivery must be adhered to. At the time of any well shut-down or mine closure, the Crown must ensure that habitat restoration has been carried out, and rescind the legislation that provided for the development. Also, the Crown, although it may have little say in where royalties are invested or spent, has an obligation to assist the Gitxsan in the negotiation of a fair rate of return, and has a role to play in assuring that the royalties are transferred to the community in accordance with any previously negotiated agreement.

Governance

Governance, for the Gitxsan, is situated in the authority of the *Simgigyet* or *Sigidim haanak'a,* which recognizes traditional *wilp* alliances and the tradition of *sisixek* — pulling the chiefs out for consultation — while maintaining individual *wilp* members' rights to be involved in any decision-making process. The *wilp* alliance is directed through the *Gim litxwid*, but there are some situations in which the *Simgigyet* or *Sigidim haanak'a* come together as family alliances or members of the same village, and as a nation to make decisions. This action of *sisixek* gives the Gitxsan their shape as an Aboriginal nation, in that it creates a body of people informed about a problem, or the need to critically examine an issue or concern. The *Gim litxwid*, depending on the issue, the location of the concern, or the degree of immediacy, will determine what percentage of Gitxsan people are necessary to form a consensus; consensus could realistically range from 40 to 80 per cent, according to ratios set by the Gitxsan people.

Wilp resource and land management is the primary concern of the *Simgigyet* or *Sigidim haanak'a*, in that any infraction that occurs on the *lax'wiiyip* is ultimately borne by them, but day-to-day management is delegated to various *wilp* members. Besides being head of the *wilp's* resource management team, the *Sigidim haanak'a* confers with her peers in order that everyone is kept apprised of all subsistence activities and the condition of the *lax'wiiyip*. The relationship of the Gitxsan with their *lax'wiiyip* through the social and management responsibilities of the *Sigidim haanak'a* lies at the heart of Gitxsan governance. Those who hold the position either inherit it from the departing *Sigidim haanak'a* or are appointed by consensus of the *wilp*. Regardless of how the *Sigidim haanak'a* achieves office, the other *Simgigyet* or *Sigidim haanak'a* must approve the appointment at a *yukw* called for the purpose.

The *Sigidim haanak'a* must make the final decisions regarding the disposition of land and resources. This does not preclude a body of advisors from among the general population, nor does it stop *wilp* members from either bringing up concerns prior to the decision, debating solutions, or being responsible to act on the decisions of the *Sigidim haanak'a*, but it must be her authority that endorses the action undertaken on the land. Thus, the shape of Gitxsan governance is firmly rooted in the *wilp*, and relies on the public role of the *Simgigyet* or *Sigidim haanak'a* to bring *wilp* concerns forward and assist *wilp* members in coming to a consensus with current business.

In terms of the administration of *wilp* resources, two questions must be considered. First, how are individual Gitxsan Section 35 rights to be met in light of the overall conservation of resources? Second, how will the authority of the *Simgigyet* or *Sigidim haanak'a* be supported, considering they have the final say on matters related to *wilp* management on their *lax'wiiyip*, they act as liaisons with provincial and federal leaders regarding Section 35 rights to resources, and they are the decision-makers with respect to alternative uses of the *wilp lax'wiiyip*?

All Gitxsan people are trained in the laws of the fishery and the hunt, and they know that permission must be sought from the *Sigidim haanak'a* to use *wilp* resources and sites. Thus, it may not be a burden to require them to report to a central office the numbers, species, and locations of animal and fish taken during the seasonal round. The Resource Management Office may use the observations of the hunters, trappers, and fishers to determine the conditions of the habitats. If their reporting is accurate and kept current, the *Simgigyet*, on the advice of the Resource Management Office, would be able to caution hunters, trappers, or fishers when they were approaching limits, as well as, over time, build up profiles of any region to predict when to stop or start hunting, trapping, or fishing.

A *Sigidim haanak'a's* behaviour is continually scrutinized by *wilp* members and others of similar rank, so she must always be cognizant of the gravity of her decision. Neither may she act outside the law. Her decisions, therefore, are made in consultation with her *wilp*, and duly witnessed. If it is a village concern, it is the *Simgigyet* or *Sigidim haanak'a* who discuss the issues, and pass on their decisions to the appropriate parties. If the issue is of concern to the Gitxsan as a whole, then as many of the *Simgigyet* or *Sigidim haanak'a* as possible, with their advisors, will debate the problem and arrive at a solution. From this consensus, the appropriate office will be authorized to notify the appropriate agency of the decision. The leadership of the *Simgigyet* or *Sigidim haanak'a* starts in the *wilp*, decides village matters, confers on issues of Gitxsan concerns, and is responsible to interface with the Crown. The long-term political success of the *Simgigyet* and *Sigidim haanak'a*, however, lies in how well they have been able to harness the labour of their *wilp* members for the benefit of the *wilp*. With this in mind, leadership success may also be contingent on how well the *Simgigyet* and *Sigidim haanak'a* are able to delegate to *wilp* members, and how the Gitxsan use funds from compensation and royalties for projects that benefit all of them.

The relationship between the Gitxsan and the Crown, both provincial and federal, centres on protection of their Section 35 rights, which are land based and associated with livelihood concerns, as well as clarity with respect to consultation. With respect to this relationship, the *Sigidim haanak'a* could easily delegate representatives from her *Gim litxwid* alliances, whose actions and conclusions would be duly witnessed by all *Simgigyet* or *Sigidim haanak'a* at a *li'ligit* organized for the occasion. For administration purposes, the Resources Management Office could act as a clearing house for information and the bringing together of the parties, as well as co-ordinate any agreed-on dispute resolution process.

Conclusion

The Gitxsan rely on their commitment to their *lax'wiiyip* as the compelling reason for taking responsibility for the stewardship and management of the territories so that, at minimum, their Section 35 rights are upheld. They are willing to accept the challenge of being co-managers of these rights in their traditional territory, in order that they are able to continue to live in the region and exercise their Aboriginal rights. The setting of joint environmental standards and indices for compensation related to resource sharing among the *huwilp*, Canada, and British Columbia, is at the heart of the Gitxsan treaty model. As such, it is imperative that Canada be prepared to support the Gitxsan when they consider that their Section 35 rights are in jeopardy. To this end, Canada could develop joint legislation with the Gitxsan and British Columbia, specifying standards for the environmental protection of Gitxsan *lax'wiiyip* in light of their Section 35 rights and supporting the fiduciary obligations of the Crown for economic development in the region, and to set criteria for legitimate legislative infringements in order to protect Aboriginal rights.

In terms of the relationship with the province, the Gitxsan and British Columbia could develop compensation indices that accommodate the Gitxsan perspective on resource development and address the sharing of revenues. There is no reason for the Gitxsan to relinquish Aboriginal title, as it is associated with their cultural identity or Indian-ness through intimate association with the *lax'wiiyip*, the *adawaaks*, and the *ayooks*. Since the assertion of sovereignty, the Gitxsan's traditional livelihood has been altered; they seek additional economic opportunities in the region as well as involvement in setting the standards for the delivery of social services.

Although the federal government insists that blanket extinguishment is no longer required as a precursor to a land claim agreement, the Crown requires certainty and finality. Current policy still requires that the community identify additional lands, including a proportion of non-traditional resources, to be defined as fee simple, and the Gitxsan people would be subject to all relevant taxes. On these fee simple lands, the Gitxsan would have exclusive control over and would be able to manage their affairs according to their own governance system. The Gitxsan community is expected to identify site-specific Aboriginal user rights throughout their traditional territories, but these activities will be subject to federal and provincial regulation, as well as Crown appropriation. What the province hopes to achieve is closure on the Aboriginal title question and certainty as to who has jurisdiction over any given Aboriginal right activities. This still translates as "cede and surrender," in that the community is expected to accept an enlarged reserve as modified entitlement lands and have access to Section 35 rights to the remainder of their traditional territories. This model prevents any meaningful or continuous relationship with the resources on or below Gitxsan traditional territories, providing little security beyond the compensation package at the time of signing. For the Gitxsan, their relationship is with their entire *lax'wiiyip*; it is where their history lives.

The Gitxsan have permitted the peaceful settlement of their *lax'wiiyip* by the *Lixs giigyet*, acknowledging that underlying sovereignty to the soil is vested in the Crown, at the expense of their own rights and livelihood. They have opened the possibility for Canada to critically examine the nature of Aboriginal property ownership and regulatory schemes, and the need to reconcile legitimate legislative imperatives and third party uses of the land and resources while protecting Aboriginal rights. The Gitxsan believe that their relationship with Canada should be based on acceptance of their distinctiveness and protection of their Section 35 rights. The Supreme Court of Canada enlarged the scope of Aboriginal title to include the possibility that the community was not required to cede its territory unless the use sought was contrary to the Indian-ness of the community. This suggests that Gitxsan jurisdictional parameters have also been expanded, and leaves room for a treaty relationship with the potential for a continued relationship with the community's entire territories that includes non-traditional use, such as forestry, mining, and oil and gas development.

The critical difference between the Gitxsan treaty model and that of the current comprehensive claims position is in the fact that the Gitxsan claim the right to manage their entire *lax'wiiyip* according to their *ayooks*, and are prepared to meet this challenge in the courtroom. They do not want a treaty that allocates to them enlarged reserves and requires them to cede access to resources and jurisdiction over the *lax'wiiyip* that has formed their identity, nor do they believe that the current reserve or village self-government model can adequately speak to the efficient delivery of their social and cultural needs while encouraging self-sufficiency. The Gitxsan believe that, both as individuals and as a group, they have obligations and duties to their *wilp*, to their kinship alliances, to their political and social alliances, and to the *lax'wiiyip*. They believe that their relationship with the Crown is situated in the Crown's respect for and recognition of their institutions, and the challenge of providing ongoing livelihoods for *wilp* members in the *lax'wiiyip*.

Although their rights of self-government have been diminished since declared sovereignty in 1846, the Gitxsan believe they retained the right to some form of self-government and self-regulation. What rights the Gitxsan would have given up in 1846 would be the capacity to declare war, impose their laws and customs on settlers or other First Nations, and such of their laws and customs that were contrary to natural justice and the moral standards of the time, which without change could not have been part of the common law. After incorporating the above changes, the civil aspects of the common law in 1846 — or even 1871 when British Columbia entered Confederation — would have been able to accommodate and protect Gitxsan self-government and self-regulation based on their customs, traditions, and practices to the extent that these aspects of Gitxsan life form an integral part of their society and their Indian-ness. This would have included any customary laws of self-government and self-regulation as it applied to the Gitxsan people in 1871. Since 1871 there has not been any clear and plain intention to abrogate them. In fact, they are, arguably, protected by Section 35 of the *Constitution Act, 1982*.

The Canadian Constitution gives Gitxsan people the opportunity to negotiate self-government based on their traditional system in areas related to their Aboriginal rights, as well as the means of managing the harvest of fish in collaboration with the Department of Fisheries and Oceans, and fur and other wildlife resources in conjunction with the provincial Ministry of the Environment. It is the role of Canada to protect Aboriginal rights, and the acknowledgement and affirmation of these rights opens the way for Canada to declare how it will act on this obligation. This, in turn, would enable British Columbia to come forward with a consultative process that would afford the Gitxsan an opportunity to respond to legitimate legislative objectives related to forestry, mining, oil and gas exploration and extraction, hydro development, the construction of transportation corridors, and enlarged settlements. This model leaves the possibility open that Gitxsan Aboriginal title remains intact. Canada would be able to fulfill its obligation, and British Columbia would have a means of interacting with the Gitxsan when it needed to infringe on the Gitxsan title for legitimate and justifiable legislative imperatives.

To affirm this ongoing commitment, the Gitxsan, Canada, and British Columbia may desire to raise a *t'saan* illustrating this renewed relationship and the terms of their commitment. Activities such as naming and applying symbolic meaning to the relationship without surrendering to one another would eliminate the need to extract the promise of finality from the Gitxsan.

Having Canada and British Columbia define their relationship to the Gitxsan, and having this relationship marked on a *t'saan* which, in itself, has a life span, begs the periodic review of the terms of the relationship among all parties. A *t'saan*, as a marker that can be read, requires literacy and continued information exchanges in order for the principles to be understood. If Canada is willing to take on a meaningful role that protects Gitxsan title and rights, which enables them to continue their relationship with their *lax'wiiyip* despite third party use, then British Columbia and all concerned can be guaranteed certainty.

Notes

Notes to Chapter One – pp. 23-28

1 *Simgigyet* refers to male hereditary chiefs, *Sigidim haanak'a* to female. This work generally favours the feminine usage.

2 *Xkyeehl* privileges are extended to individuals for access to resource locations after they have offered items of equal value to the *wilp* in question. M. McKenzie, Proceedings at Trial (1987) vol. 7, May 20, at 383, 418-419; and A. Mathews, Proceedings at Trial (1988) vol. 76, March 17, at 4721-4722.

3 Gitxsan and British Columbia, *A Reconciliation Agreement between Her Majesty the Queen in Right of British Columbia and the Hereditary Chiefs of the Gitxsan*, Sept. 14, 1998.

4 *R. v. Van der Peet* [1996] 2 S.C.R. 507.

5 P. Cumming and N. Mickenberg, *Native Rights in Canada*, 2nd ed. (Toronto: Indian-Eskimo Association of Canada, 1972).

6 R. S. Allen, *His Majesty's Indian Allies: British Indian Policy in the Defence of Canada, 1774 to 1815* (Toronto: Dundurn Press, 1992).

7 W. C. Wicken, *Mi'Kmaq Treaties on Trial: History, Land and Donald Marshall Junior* (Toronto: University of Toronto Press, 2001).

8 A. J. Ray, J. R. Miller, and F. Tough, *Bounty and Benevolence: A History of Saskatchewan Treaties* (Montreal: McGill-Queen's University Press, 2000).

9 B. Slattery, "Understanding Aboriginal Rights" (1987) 66 *Canadian Bar Review*, 727.

10 R. Preston, *Cree Narrative*, 2nd ed. (Montreal: McGill-Queens Press, 2002), p. 212.

11 F. G. Speck, "Penobscot Tales and Religious Beliefs," *Journal of American Folklore*, vol. 48, no. 187 (1935): 1-107, at 13.

12 S. Rushford, *Bear Lake Athapaskan Kinship and Task Formation* (Ottawa: National Museum of Man, 1984), p. 38

13   P. R. Coutu and L. Hoffman-Mercredi, *Ikonze: The Stones of Traditional Knowledge: A History of Northeastern Alberta* (Edmonton: Thunderwoman Ethnographics, 1999).

14   K. Rasmussen, "Iglulik and Caribou Eskimo Texts," in *Report of the Fifth Thule Expedition, 1921-1924*, vol. 3 (Copenhagen: 1930), p. 498.

15   *Delgam'Uukw (Muldoe) et al.* v. *R. in Right of British Columbia and Attorney General of Canada* [1997] 3 S.C.R. 1010.

16   *Haida Nation* v. *British Columbia (Minister of Forests)* [2004] 3 S.C.R. 511.

17   *Mikisew Cree First Nation* v. *Canada (Minister of Canadian Heritage)* [2005] 3 S.C.R. 388.

18   *Haida, supra* note 16 at para. 45.

Notes to Chapter Two – pp. 29-54

1   Discussed in detail in Chapter 4, the *adawaaks* record *wilp* origins, migrations, and the boundaries of the *lax'wiiyip* of each *wilp*. See Olive Ryan, "The First *Adawaak* of *Antgulilbix*," Proceedings at Trial (1987), vol. 17, Jun. 11 at 112-17.

2   M. Johnson, The *Adawaak* of *Tsibasaa* and *Antgulilbix*, Proceedings at Trial (1987), vol. 11, May 27 at 665-68.

3   The *Adawaak* of *Haat'ixslaxnox* (Johnson, *supra* note 2 at 666 -70).

4   F. Boas, *Tsimshian Mythology* (Washington, DC: Smithsonian Institution, 31 Annual Report for the Bureau of American Ethnology for the Years 1909-10, 1916) at 106-08.

5   There used to be one language at *T'am Laxa mit* before they used the *Tsimxsan* language. They called this *sim algyax* and now the Gitxsan use what is known as *gyanimx*. Johnson, *supra* note 2 at 668.

6   F. W. Howay, "An Outline of the Maritime Fur Trade," *Report of the Canadian Historical Association, 1932*, p. 147.

7   J. A. McDonald, *Trying to Make a Life: The Historical Political Economy of the Kitsumalum*, Unpublished PhD Dissertation (University of British Columbia: Department of Anthropology and Sociology, 1985).

8   A. J. Ray, "Fur Trade History and the Gitksan-Wet'suwet'en Comprehensive Claim: Men of Property and the Exercise of Title," in K. Abel and J. Friesen (Eds.), *Aboriginal Resource Use in Canada: Historical and Legal Aspects* (Winnipeg: University of Manitoba Press, 1991), p. 303.

9   A. J. Ray, "The Early Economic History of the Gitksan-Wet'suwet'en-Babine Tribal Territories, 1822-1915," prepared for the Gitksan-Wet'suwet'en Tribal Council, 16 Jan. 1985, pp. 2-7.

10   R. M. Galois and S. Marsden, "The Tsimshian, the Hudson's Bay Company, and the Geopolitics of the Northwest Coast Fur Trade, 1787–1840," *Canadian Geographer* 39 (1995): 169-183.

11   A. Ray, Proceedings at Trial (1989), vol. 203, Mar. 21, at 13466-13467.

12   *Treaty between Her Majesty and the United States of America, for the settlement of the Oregon Boundary* (Washington, DC: 15 Jun. 1846).

13   H. Meilleur, *A Pour of Rain: Stories from a West Coast Fort* (Victoria: Sono Nis Press, 1980), p. 157.

14   Major W. Downie, "1859 gold explorations, report by Mr. W. Downie of his journey to Queen Charlotte's Island, and thence by Fort Simpson to the interior of British Columbia," in *Further Papers relative to the Affairs of British Columbia, Part III – Copies of Dispatches from the Governor of British Columbia to the Secretary of State for the Colonies, and from the Secretary of State to the Governor, Relative to the Government of the Colony* (London: Queen's Printers, 1860) pp. 71-73.

15   R. M. Galois, "The History of the Upper Skeena Region, 1850 to 1927," *Native Studies Review* 2 (1993-94): 142.

16   C. Mackay, "The Collins Overland Telegraph," *British Columbia Historical Quarterly* 10 (1946): 212-13.

17   J. A. McDonald, "Images of the Nineteenth Century Economy of the Tsimshian," in M. Sequin (Ed.), *The Tsimshian: Images of the Past, Views of the Present* (Vancouver: University of British Columbia Press, 1984), pp. 40-44.

18   Rev. D. Jennings, *The Missionary Outlook* (Spring 1893), p. 33.

19   "Petition of Indians at Kitesgoually to Lieutenant Governor," National Archives of Canada, RG 10, vol. 1159, n.p.

20   Editorial, Victoria *Daily Colonist* (9 Jul. 1872), n.p.

21   R. M. Galois, "The Burning of Kitsegukla, 1872," *BC Studies* 94 (1992): 59-81.

22   A. W. Humphrey, Diary, Jun. 7, 1874 (British Columbia Archives and Records Service, E/C/H 881).

23   E. Pettingell, Statement, Sept. 18, 1874, Church Missionary Society, "Duncan Papers," University of British Columbia Archives, 16055.

24   Rev. Robert Tomlinson, "Journal, 1874," Church Missionary Society, vol. 106, #143.

25   H. Foster, "The Queen's Law is Better than Yours: International Homicide in Early British Columbia," in J. Phillips et al. (Eds.), *Essays in the History of Canadian Law*, vol. 5, *Crime and Criminal Justice* (Toronto: University of Toronto Press, 1994), p. 41.

26   "An Eye for an Eye," Victoria *Daily Colonist* (21 Jun. 1884), n.p.

27   "Chiefs of Kitseguecla," Victoria *Daily Colonist* (7 Sept. 1884), n.p.

28   Editorial, *supra* note 26.

29   "Kitwancool Jim," Victoria *Daily Colonist* (7 Nov. 1888), n.p.

30   W. H. Pierce, *From Potlatch to Pulpit: Being the Autobiography of the Rev. William Henry Pierce, Native Missionary to the Indian Tribes of the Northwest Coast of British Columbia* (Vancouver, 1933), pp. 58-59; and W. H. Pierce, "Evils of Indian Witchcraft," *The Western Recorder* (May 1928): 8.

31   N. Fitzstubbs, "Proceedings at Hazelton, 18 Oct. 1888," National Archives of Canada, RG 10, vol. 3802, file 49774.

32   Editorial, Victoria *Daily Colonist* (21 Jun. 1884), n.p.

33   Department of Indian Affairs, *Annual Report, 1889*.

34   R. Mackie, "The Colonization of Vancouver Island, 1849-1858" *BC Studies* 96 (1992/1993): 3 at 4.

35   A. Barclay, 17 Dec. 1849, A.6/28 folio: 90d-92, Hudson's Bay Archives.

36   See "Conveyances of Land to the Hudson's Bay Company by Indian Tribes," in *Papers Connected with the Indian Land Question, 1850 to 1875* (Victoria: Queen's Printer, 1875), pp. 5-11.

37   R. E. Cail, *Land, Man and the Law: The Disposal of Crown Lands in British Columbia, 1871-1913* (Vancouver: University of British Columbia, 1974); R. Fisher, *Contact and Conflict: Indian-European Relations in British Columbia, 1774-1890* (Vancouver: University of British Columbia Press, 1977); and P. Tennant, *Aboriginal Peoples and Politics: The Indian Land Question in British Columbia, 1849 to 1989* (Vancouver: University of British Columbia Press, 1991).

38   W. J. McKay, "Report of the Kamloops Agency," *Annual Report of the Department of Indian Affairs, 1885*, Sessional Papers, vol. 19(4) (49 Victoria) (Ottawa: Department of Indian Affairs, 1886), n.p.

39 House of Assembly, 28 Jan. 1860, British *Colonist* (29 Jan. 1861).

40 Editorial, *supra* note 26.

41 J. Douglas, 14 Mar. 1859, *Papers Connected with the Indian Land Question, supra* note 36 at 16-17.

42 *Ibid.*

43 W. Duff, "The Fort Victoria Treaties" *BC Studies* 3 (1969): 3.

44 *Ibid.*, p. 17.

45 I. W. Powell to the Provincial Secretary, Department of Indian Affairs, 15 Aug. 1874, *supra* note 36, pp. 139-140.

46 K. Brealey, "Travels from Point Ellice: Peter O'Reilly and the Indian Reserve System in British Columbia," *BC Studies* 115 and 116 (1997-98): 181-85.

47 Fisher, *supra* note 37 at 9.

48 J. Trutch, "Report of Lands and Works Department, Enclosure: Lower Fraser River Indian Reserves," 28 Aug. 1867, p. 42.

49 I. Powell, P. O'Reilly, and G. Vernon to Chief Isadore and the Kootenay Indians, 10 Oct. 1887, British Columbia, *Reserve Allocation Commission Annual Report, 1887.*

50 R. Fisher, "Joseph Trutch and Indian Land Policy," *BC Studies* 12 (1971-72): 16-19.

51 Fisher, *supra* note 37 at 157.

52 J. W. Trutch to W. Moberly, 10 Oct. 1865, GR 1372 (Reel B-1351).

53 J. W. Trutch, "Report of the Lower Fraser Indian Reserve," 28 Aug. 1867, *supra* note 36 at 41-43.

54 J. W. Trutch, "Report of the Government of British Columbia on the Subject of Indian Reserves," 29 Jan. 1870, *supra* note 36 at 11.

55 British Columbia Legislative Council, "Debate on the Subject of Confederation with Canada," reprinted from the *Government Gazette Extraordinary*, Mar. 1870 (Victoria: Queen's Printer, 1870), pp. 146-147.

56 Cail, *supra* note 37 at 187.

57 Report of the Government of British Columbia on the subject of Indian Reserves, 17 Aug. 1875, *supra* note 36, Appendix at 1.

58 D. Laird, Memorandum, 2 Nov. 1874, *ibid.* at 152.

59 J. W. Trutch to J. A. Macdonald, in J. Pope, *Correspondence of Sir John Macdonald: Selections from the Correspondence of Sir John Alexander Macdonald, G.C.B., First Prime Minister of Canada* (Toronto: Oxford University Press, 1921), p. 185.

60 T. Fournier, "Report of the Honourable Minister of Justice, approved by His Excellency the Governor General in Council, 23 Jan. 1875" in W. E. Hodgins (Comp.), *Correspondence: Reports of the Ministers of Justice and Order in Council upon the Subject of Dominion and Provincial Legislation, 1867-1920* (Ottawa: Government Printing Bureau, 1896-1922), pp. 1:1024-1:1025.

61 *Ibid.*

62 Tennant, *supra* note 37 at 41.

63 R. W. Scott, Memorandum from the Minister of the Interior, 5 Nov. 1875, *supra* note 36 at 161.

64 Brealey, *supra* note 49 at 186.

65 Scott, *supra* note 36 at 163.

66 Douglas, *supra* note 36 at 16-17.

67 P. Patterson, "Decade of Change: Origins of the Nisgha and Tsimshian Land Protests in the 1880s," *Journal of Canadian Studies* 18(3) (1983): 44.

68 S. Rush, Proceedings at Trial (1987), vol. 2, May 11 at 70.

69 *Ibid.*

70 R. Tomlinson to the Provincial Secretary, 20 Oct. 1884, in R. Galois, Proceedings at Trial (1989), vol. 226, May 18 at 16459.

71 N. Fitzstubbs to C. W. D. Clifford, National Archives of Canada, RG 10, vol. 3628, file 6244-1; and N. Fitzstubbs to Attorney General, 5 Jan. 1889, National Archives of Canada, Babine Agency Letter-book, RG 10, vol. 1585.

72 C. F. Roth, "Goods, Names, and Selves: Rethinking the Tsimshian Potlatch," *American Ethnologist* 29 (1) (2002): 123; D. Cole and I. Chaikin, *An Iron Hand Upon the People: The Law Against the Potlatch on the Northwest Coast* (Vancouver: Douglas & McIntyre, 1990).

73 R. E. Loring to A. W. Vowell, 15 Jul. 1897, National Archives of Canada, Babine Agency Letter-book, RG 10, vol. 1585.

74 R. Galois, Proceedings at Trial (1989), vol. 227, May 19 at 16556-16558.

75 "Indian Unrest," Vancouver *Province*, 16 Jul. 1909.

76 Galois, *supra* note 15 at 151.

77　J. McDougall to McLean, 21 Sept. 1909, National Archives of Canada, RG 10, vol. 7786, file 27151-1.

78　J. McDougall to Oliver, 11 Mar. 1911, National Archives of Canada, RG 10 vol. 4020, file 280 at 470-472.

79　*British Columbia Gazette*, 27 Dec. 1907 at 8695.

80　Special Joint Committee of the Senate and House of Commons Appointed to Inquire in the Claims of the Allied Tribes of British Columbia, as set forth by their Petition submitted to Parliament in 1927, Report and Evidence, Appendix to the *Journal of the Senate of the Canada*, First Session of the Sixteenth Parliament, 1926-27 (Ottawa: King's Printer, 1927), p. 53.

81　Cail, *supra* note 37 at 236-37.

82　Tennant, *supra* note 37 at 96-124.

83　C. M. Tate, Circular Letter, 16 Dec. 1912, National Archives of Canada, RG 10, vol. 11023, file 662.

84　*Proceedings of the Royal Commission on Indian Affairs for the Province of British Columbia*, Meeting with the Kuldoe Band or Tribe of Indians at Hazelton on Tuesday, 13 Jul. 1915, p. 1.

85　"Statement of the United Tribes of Northern British Columbia for the Government of Canada," 27 Feb. 1919.

86　Special Joint Committee, *supra* note 80 at 50-51.

87　*An Act to Amend the Indian Act*, S.C. (1926 -27) c. 32 (17 Geo. V) at pt. 149.

Notes to Chapter Three – pp. 55-84

1　K. Muldoe and A. Joseph, Proceedings at Trial (1987), vol. 2, May 11, at 66-67.

2　H. B. Hawthorne (Ed.), *Survey of the Contemporary Indians of Canada: Economic, Political, Educational Needs and Policies*, vol. 1 and 2 (Ottawa: Department of Indian Affairs and Northern Development, 1966).

3　*Statement of the Government of Canada on Indian Policy, 1969* (Ottawa: Department of Indian Affairs, 1969).

4　Department of Indian Affairs and Northern Development, *Outstanding Business: A Native Claims Policy, Specific Claims* (Ottawa: Ministry of Supply and Services, 1982).

5　*Calder* v. *the Attorney General of British Columbia* [1973] S.C.R. 313 at 402.

6   *Re Paulette et al. and Registrar of Titles* (No. 2) [1973] 6 W.W.R. 97.

7   *La societé de développment de la Baie James,* [1975] R.J.Q. 166.

8   *Agreement between the Government of Quebec, Grand Council of the Crees (of Quebec) and Northern Quebec Inuit Association and the Government of Canada* (Ottawa: Department of Indian and Northern Affairs, 1975).

9   Department of Indian Affairs and Northern Development, *In All Fairness: A Native Claims Policy, Comprehensive Claims* (Ottawa: Ministry of Supply and Services, 1981).

10   Statement made by the Honourable Jean Chrétien, Minister of Indian Affairs and Northern Development on Claims of Indian and Inuit People, August 8, 1973, p. 2.

11   *Ibid., at* 4- 5.

12   *Gitksan-Carrier Declaration,* Kispiox, BC, 7 Nov. 1977.

13   *Response of the Government of British Columbia to the Position Paper of the Nishga Tribal Council,* 10 Jan. 1978.

14   Hawthorne Report, *supra* note 2 at 1: 211-34.

15   G. Williams, Proceedings at Trial (1988) vol. 107, June 1 at 6761-69.

16   A. Mathews, Proceedings at Trial (1988) vol. 76, March 16 at 4695.

17   J. Douglas to the Duke of Newcastle, 25 March 1861, *Papers Connected with the Indian Land Question,* p. 19.

18   *Delgam'Uukw (Muldoe) et al. v. R. in Right of British Columbia and Attorney General of Canada* [1991] 3 W.W.R. 97.

19   *Hamlet of Baker Lake (et al.) v. Minister of Indian Affairs and Northern Development (et al.)* (1979), 107 D.L.R. (3rd) at 542.

20   *Delgam'Uukw* 1991, *supra* note 18 at 117.

21   *Ibid., at* 387-88.

22   *Calder, supra* note 5.

23   *Ibid., at* 425.

24   *Delgam'Uukw* 1991, *supra* note 18 at 177.

25   *Ibid., at* 117-18; 371-74.

26   A. Ray, Proceedings at Trial (1988) vol. 203, March 21 at 13427-13428.

27 *Delgam'Uukw* 1991, *supra* note 18 at 203-04.

28 *Ibid.*, at 178.

29 *Uukw et al.* v. *R. in Right of British Columbia and the Attorney General of Canada* [1988] 1 C.N.L.R. 188.

30 *Delgam'Uukw* 1991, *supra* note 18 at 175-82.

31 *Delgam'Uukw (Muldoe) et al.* v. *R. in right of British Columbia and Attorney General of Canada* [1997] 3 S.C.R. 1010 at 1065-1079.

32 F. Boas, *Tsimshian Mythology*, Annual Report for the Bureau of American Ethnology for the Years 1909-10 (Washington, DC: Smithsonian Institution, 1916).

33 J. Cove and G. F. MacDonald (Eds.), *Tsimshian Narratives*, vol. I and II, collected by Marius Barbeau and William Beynon (Ottawa: Canadian Museum of Civilization, 1987).

34 J. Cove, *Shattered Images: Dialogues and Meditations on Tsimshian Narratives* (Ottawa: Carleton University Press, 1987), pp. 49-156.

35 M.-F. Guedon, quoted in C. Faber, "Afterwards: Time in a Box," in M. Sequin (Ed.), *Tsimshian: Images of the Past, Views from the Present* (Vancouver: University of British Columbia Press, 1984), p. 309.

36 *Delgam'Uukw* 1991, *supra* note 18 at 179.

37 *Ibid.*, at 443.

38 M. McKenzie, Proceedings at Trial (1987), vol. 8, May 21 at 468.

39 O. Ryan, Proceedings at Trial (1987), vol. 17, June 11 at 1111-1123.

40 M. Brown, Commissioned Evidence (1985), vol. 2, Sept. 19 at 22 -25.

41 G. Williams, Proceedings at Trial (1988), vol. 105, May 30 at 6632-6634.

42 *Delgam'Uukw* 1991, *supra* note 18 at 128.

43 *Ibid.*, at 407.

44 *Ibid.*, at 408.

45 *Ibid.*, at 379.

46 *Ibid.*, at 380.

47 M. Walters, "British Imperial Constitutional Law and Aboriginal Rights: A Comment on *Delgam'Uukw* v. *British Columbia*" (1992) 17 Queen's L.J. 350.

48 *Delgam'Uukw (Muldoe) et al.* v. *R. in right of British Columbia and Attorney General of Canada* [1993] 5 W.W.R. 97.

49 M. McCullough, "Laying Down the Law: The Gitksan Decision Reinforces Government Indian Policy," *British Columbia Report: The Weekly Newsmagazine* (1991) 2 (30): 10.

50 *Ibid.*

51 *British Columbia Treaty Commission Act,* 1995 c. 45.

52 T. Molloy, *The World is Our Witness: The Historic Journey of the Nisga'a into Canada* (Calgary: Fifth House, 2000), pp. 62-63.

53 L. Dolha, "Province Recognizes 'Political Legitimacy'," *Kahtou: The Voice of BC's First Nations* 10 (1) (1992): 1-2

54 *Delgam'Uukw* 1993, *supra* note 48 at 99 to 100.

55 *Ibid.,* at 178, para. 279.

56 *Ibid.,* at 128-129, para. 65-66.

57 *Ibid.,* at 178, para. 281.

58 R. Freedman, "The Space for Aboriginal Self-Government in British Columbia: The Effect of the Decision of the British Columbia Court of Appeal in *Delgamuukw* v. *British Columbia*" (1994) 28(1) *UBC Law Review,* 51.

59 *Delgam'Uukw,* 1993, *supra* note 48 at 151, para. 165.

60 *Ibid.,* at 153, para. 174.

61 *Ibid.,* at 224, para. 478.

62 *Ibid.,* at 99.

63 *Ibid.,* at 275, para. 659-660.

64 *Ibid.,* at 274, para. 656.

65 *Ibid.,* at 290, para. 721.

66 *Ibid.,* at 273, para. 654.

67 *Ibid.,* at 277, para. 666.

68 *R.* v. *Sparrow* [1990] 1 S.C.R. 1075 at 1110.

69 *Sparrow, supra* note 68 at 1099.

70 *Delgam'Uukw* 1993, *supra* note 48 at 277-278, para. 669.

71   *Ibid.,* at 350, para. 971.

72   *Ibid.,* at 363 para. 1029.

73   *Ibid.,* at 100.

74   An Accord of Recognition and Respect, 13 June 1994. The Accord was renewed in July 1995.

75   "Substantive Issues, Draft Three," 15 Jan. 1996 (Hazelton: Gitxsan Hereditary Chiefs Office, 1996).

76   A. Robinson, "Fact Finder's Report on the Suspension of the Gitxsan Treaty Negotiations" (Vancouver: British Columbia Treaty Commission, 1996): 7.

77   J. Cashore to D. Ryan, 1 Feb. 1996 (Victoria: Ministry of Aboriginal Affairs File no. 63300-20/Gitx/COR, 1996).

78   Robinson, *supra* note 76 at 9.

79   *Delgam'Uukw* 1993, *supra* note 48 at 176-182.

80   "Playing Some Pre-election Hard Ball: The NDP Suddenly Adopts a Tough Line in Nisgha and Gitksan Treaty Talks," *British Columbia Report: The Weekly News-magazine* 7 (24) (1996): 9.

81   *Delgam'Uukw,* 1997, *supra* note 31.

Notes to Chapter Four – pp. 85-124

1   S. Marsden, Proceedings at Trial (1989), vol. 232, June 5 at 17104.

2   The name *Tenmigyet* at the time of the trial was held by Arthur Mathews. A. Mathews, Proceedings at Trial (1988), vol. 73, March 14 at 4587-4589.

3   G. Wilson, *The Land Rights of Individuals Among the Nyakyusa* (Rhodes-Living-stone Papers, 1938), p. 39.

4   M. Gluckman, *Ideas in Barotse Jurisprudence* (New Haven: Yale University Press, 1965), p. 79.

5   R. H. Lowie, *Primitive Society* (London: Routledge 1921), p. 201.

6   At the filing of the statement of claim on 24 Oct. 1884, the Gitxsan name of *Delgam'Uukw* was held by Albert Tait; in Jan. 1987 the name was passed on to Ken Muldoe; near the end of the trial, the name was given to Earl Muldoe after Ken Muldoe passed away on 8 April 1990. The Wet'suwet'en name of *Gisday Wa,* at the time of the trial, was held by Alfred Joseph.

7   K. Muldoe and A. Joseph, Proceedings at Trial (1987), vol. 2, May 11 at 65-66.

8   At the time of the trial, the name *Gyologyet* was held by Mary McKenzie. M. McKenzie, Proceedings at Trial (1987), vol. 3, May 13 at 160, and 186-189

9   *Ibid.,* at 185.

10   At the time of the trial, the name *Xamlaxyeltxw* was held by Solomon Mardsen. S. Marsden, Proceedings at Trial (1988), vol. 92, May 5 at 5870, and vol. 93, May 6 at 5922.

11   At the time of the trial, the name *Ax Gwin Desxw* was held by Glen Williams. G. Williams, Proceedings at Trial (1988), vol. 105, May 6 at 6627 and 6672.

12   At the time of the trial, the name *Hanamuxw* was held by Joan Ryan. J. Ryan, Proceedings at Trial (1988), vol. 79, March 23 at 4975, and vol. 80 March 23 at 5017 and 5026.

13   S. Marsden, Proceedings at Trial (1988), vol. 94, May 9 at 5963-5964.

14   M. McKenzie, Proceedings at Trial (1987), vol. 4 May 13 at 243.

15   *Ibid.,* at 218.

16   At the time of the trial, the name *Xhliimlaxha* was held by Martha Brown. M. Brown, Commissioned Evidence (1985), vol. 1, Sept. 18 at 1, and vol. 3, Sept. 21 at 5.

17   A. Mathews, correspondence, 10 April 1999.

18   P. Muldoe, Proceedings at Trial (1988), vol. 100, May 19 at 6310.

19   Mathews, *supra* note 2 at 4513 and 4561.

20   The name *Txaaxwok* at the time of the trial was held by James Morrison. J. Morrison, Proceedings at Trial (1988), vol. 82, April 18 at 5080 and 5133.

21   A. Mathews, Proceedings at Trial (1989), vol. 76, March 17 at 4723-4724.

22   In conversation with J. Ryan, 15 Aug. 2000.

23   In conversation with A. Mathews, 18 Aug. 2000.

24   A. Mathews, Proceedings at Trial (1989), vol. 74, March 15 at 4607.

25   O. Ryan, Proceedings at Trial (1987), vol. 17, June 11 at 1134.

26   S. Williams, Commissioned Evidence (1988), vol. 2, April 18 at 198.

27   *Ibid.,* at 168.

28   Marsden, *supra* note 13 at 5956-5957.

29 *Ibid.,* at 5938-5939.

30 M. McKenzie, Proceedings at Trial (1987), vol. 6, May 19 at 361.

31 Brown, *supra* note 16 at 20.

32 Mathews, *supra* note 21 at 4720-4723.

33 Marsden, *supra* note 13 at 5948.

34 *Ibid.,* at 5940-5941.

35 Williams, *supra* note 11 at 6646-6647.

36 Mathews, *supra* note 2 at 4557.

37 Mathews, *supra* note 24 at 4643.

38 A. Mathews, Proceedings at Trial (1987), vol. 75, March 16 at 4671.

39 Mathews, *supra* note 21 at 4776.

40 *Ibid.,* at 4721-4722.

41 J. Morrison, Proceedings at Trial, (1988), vol. 83, April 19 at 5170-5171; 5244.

42 McKenzie, *supra* note 8 at 249.

43 At the time of the trial, the name *Gwaans* was held by Olive Ryan. O. Ryan, Proceedings at Trial (1987), vol. 16, June 10 at 1013, and vol. 19, June 15 at 1249-1251.

44 At the time of the trial, the name *Antgulilbix* was held by Mary Johnson. M. Johnson, Proceedings at Trial (1987), vol. 10, May 26 at 616, and vol. 13, May 29 at 800-801.

45 At the time of the trial, the name *Lelt* was held by Fred Johnson. F. Johnson, Commissioned Evidence (1986), vol. 1, Sept. 2 at 1 and 59-61.

46 Johnson, *supra* note 44 at 748.

47 Mathews, *supra* note 24 at 4582.

48 *Ibid.,* at 4565-4566.

49 S. Marsden, Proceedings at Trial (1988), vol. 93, May 6 at 5911.

50 Ryan, *supra* note 12 at 4982.

51 M. McKenzie, Proceedings at Trial (1987), vol. 5, May 15 at 311-312.

52 Ryan, *supra* note 12 at 5006-5007.

53 G. Williams, Proceedings at Trial (1988), vol. 107, June 1 at 6812.

54 At the time of the trial, the name *Gitludahl* was held by Peter Muldoe. P. Muldoe, Proceedings at Trial (1988), vol. 97, May 16 at 6090 and 6113.

55 Mathews, *supra* note 21 at 4756.

56 McKenzie. *supra* note 51 at 353-354.

57 There are various ranks of *Sigidim haanak'a*, and a *Xsgooim* holds the authority to delegate to other persons who are designated as *Hli Kaaxhl*. The rank and *wilp* affiliation of a *Sigidim haanak'a* is shown by the seating order at a *yukw*.

58 McKenzie, *supra* note 30 at 366.

59 *Ibid.*, at 367.

60 Mathews, *supra* note 21 at 4756-4757.

61 *Ibid.*, at 4756.

62 Ryan, *supra* note 12 at 5013.

63 G. Williams, Proceedings at Trial (1988), vol. 106, May 31 at 6716.

64 R. Daly, *"Our Box Was Full": Ethnography of the Plaintiffs* (Vancouver: University of British Columbia Press, 2004), p. 271.

65 Ryan, *supra* note 12 at 5007.

66 Mathews, *supra* note 24 at 4651-4660.

67 A. Mathews in R. Daly, Proceedings at Trial (1989), vol. 187, Feb. 23 at 12086-12087.

68 Literally, "They fought over the kill of a caribou." Mathews, *supra* note 2 at 4586.

69 *Ibid.*, at 4588.

70 Mathews, *supra* note 38 at 4668-4669.

71 Muldoe, *supra* note 18 at 6310.

72 Morrison, *supra* note 41 at 5234-5235.

73 M. McKenzie, Proceedings at Trial (1987), vol. 8, May 21 at 441-442.

74 *Ibid.*, at 462-463.

75 J. Morrison, Proceedings at Trial (1988), vol. 84, April 20 at 5287 and 5300.

76 Morrison, *supra* note 20 at 5123-5124

77 V. Smith, Proceedings at Trial (1988) vol. 89, May 2 at 5616 and 5665.

78 At the time of the trial, the name of *Sakxum Higookx* was held by Vernon Smith. V. Smith, Proceedings at Trial, (1988) vol. 89 May 2 at 5665.

79 Williams, *supra* note 53 at 6815.

80 *Ibid.,* at 6818-6820.

81 McKenzie, *supra* note 51 at 294.

82 R. Daly, *"Our Box Was Full": The Gitksan-Wet'suwet'en Economy.* Opinion Evidence, June 1987 at 100.

83 *Ibid.,* at 64.

Notes to Chapter Five – pp. 125-148

1 *Delgam'Uukw (Muldoe) et al.* v. *R. in Right of British Columbia and Attorney General of Canada* [1991] 3 W.W.R. 97; [1993] 5 W.W.R. 97; [1997] 3 S.C.R. 1010.

2 *R.* v. *Sparrow* [1990] 1 S.C.R. 1075; *Guerin* v. *the Queen* [1984] 2 S.C.R. 335; and *R.* v. *Van der Peet* [1996] 2 S.R.C. 507.

3 Department of Indian Affairs and Northern Development, *In All Fairness: A Native Claims Policy, Comprehensive Claims* (Ottawa: Ministry of Supply and Services, 1981).

4 Memorandum of Understanding between Canada and British Columbia Respecting the Sharing of Pre-treaty Costs, Settlement Costs, Implementation Costs and the Costs of Self-Government, 21 June 1993.

5 Lheidli T'enneh Agreement-in-Principle, 2 May 2003. (As of 3 April 2007, the Final Agreement had not been ratified.)

6 *Van der Peet, supra* note 2.

7 *Statement of the Government of Canada on Indian Policy, 1969* (Ottawa: Department of Indian Affairs, 1969).

8 *Calder* v. *British Columbia (Attorney General)* [1973] S.C.R. 313.

9 *Re Paulette et al and Registrar of Titles* (No 2) [1973] 6 W.W.R. 97.

10 *La societé de développement de la Baie James* [1975] R.J.Q. 166.

11 *Guerin, supra* note 2.

12　*Sparrow, supra* note 2 at 1119.

13　Quebec, Grand Council of the Crees (of Quebec) and Northern Quebec Inuit Association and Canada, Agreement between the Government of Quebec, Grand Council of the Crees (of Quebec) and Northern Quebec Inuit Association and the Government of Canada (Ottawa: Department of Indian and Northern Affairs, 1975).

14　Thomas R. Berger, *Northern Frontier, Northern Homeland: The Report of the Mackenzie Valley Pipeline Inquiry* (Ottawa: Minister of Supply and Services Canada, 1977*)*.

15　The Western Arctic Claim: The Inuvialuit Final Agreement (Ottawa: Department of Indian and Northern Affairs, 1984).

16　Agreement between the Inuit of the Nunavut Settlement Area and Her Majesty the Queen in Right of Canada (Ottawa: Department of Indian Affairs and Northern Development, 1993).

17　Canada, Discussion Paper on Indian Land Claims in BC (Prince George: Department of Indian and Northern Affairs for the Conference on Aboriginal Rights, 22-24 Sept. 1978).

18　Statement made by the Honourable Jean Chrétien, Minister of Indian Affairs and Northern Development on Claims of Indian and Inuit People, 8 Aug. 1973.

19　T. Glavin, "BC Joins Indians, Feds for Land Talks," *Vancouver Sun* (21 Mar. 1991), B7.

20　Nisga'a Final Agreement (Ottawa: Department of Indian and Northern Affairs, 1999).

21　*An Act for conferring certain privileges on the more Advanced Bands of the Indians of Canada* S.C. (47 Vict. c. 27 1884).

22　Conversation with P. Stewart, Deacon of Christ Church, Kincolith, 10 July 2003; and with B. McKay, 10 July 2003.

23　Quoted in O. Lippert, "Assessing the *Delgam'Uukw* Decision: A Law and Economic Perspective" (Ottawa: The Fraser Institute, 1998) at 11.6.

24　R. Howard, "BC Land Offer to Natives Small: Target of Less than 5 per cent Sharply Sour Expectations in Band's Claim," *Globe and Mail* (18 May 1995), A1 and A2.

25　Memorandum of Understanding, *supra* note 4 at Annex A at A-2 to A-3, and Annex C at C-1 to C-11.

26 The Supreme Court determined that the Crown has a duty to consult when Aboriginal title and rights are going to be infringed on, before the conclusion of a treaty. See: *Haida Nation* v. *British Columbia (Minister of Forests)* [2004] 3 S.C.R. 511; and *Taku River Tlingit First Nation* v. *British Columbia (Project Assessment Director)*, [2004] 3 S.C.R. 550.

27 Memorandum of Understanding, *supra* note 4 at 4 pt. 11.10-5 pt. 1.15.

28 *Ibid.,* at 5 pt. 1.16; 6 pt. 2.1-2.4; and 7 pt.2.6-2.10.

29 The *Gim litxwid* are alliances among the *Simgigyet* and *Sigidim haanak'a* that take into account all relationships, ranging from direct kin, persons related by *pteex*, families that have forged political relationships, past and present, and through the temporary right of *amnigwootxw* (privileged rights for children to access resources on their father's *lax'wiiyip* or for good deeds to the *wilp*). In conversation with D. Ryan, 29 Jan. 2004.

30 Gitxsan and British Columbia, A Reconciliation Agreement between Her Majesty the Queen in Right of British Columbia and the Hereditary Chiefs of the Gitxsan, Sept. 15, 1998.

31 *Ibid.,* at 4 pt. 8 through 9.

32 *Ibid.,* at 3 pt. 6 a, b and 7. a, c, d.

33 *Ibid.,* at 4 pt. 10 a - i, ii, iii; b – iv, v.

34 *Ibid.,* at 3 pt. 6 e.

35 *Ibid.,* at 4 pt. 8 a.

36 See Department of Fisheries and Oceans, "Strengthening Our Relationship: The Aboriginal Fisheries and Beyond" (Ottawa: Ministry of Supply and Services, 2002).

37 R. Michell, "The Gitksan-Wet'suwet'en Blanket Trapline Proposal," submitted to the Department of Fish and Wildlife (Hagwilget, BC: 19 Feb. 1985).

38 *Delagm'Uukw* 1997, *supra* note 1 at 1111, para. 165.

39 A Co-operative Agreement to Plan and Manage Forest Use, 2 July 1998 at 2.

40 *Ibid.,* at 3 pt. 5.1.5.

41 *Ibid.,* at 5 pt. 7.4.b.

42 *Ibid.,* at 5 pt. 7.4.c.

43 *Ibid.,* at 6 pt. 7.7.

44 *Ibid.*, at 8 pt. 12.2 to 12.4.

45 *Ibid.*, at 6 to 7 pt. 8.

46 *First Nations Commercial and Industrial Development Act* (2005, c.53).

47 In conversation with D. Ryan, 29 Jan. 2004.

Bibliography

Books and Articles

Abel, K., and J. Friesen (Eds.), *Aboriginal Resource Use in Canada: Historical and Legal Aspects* (Winnipeg: University of Manitoba Press, 1991).

Allen, R. S., *His Majesty's Indian Allies: British Indian Policy in the Defence of Canada, 1774 – 1815* (Toronto: Dundurn Press, 1992).

Berger, Thomas R., *Northern Frontier, Northern Homeland: The Report of the Mackenzie Valley Pipeline Inquiry* (Ottawa: Minister of Supply and Services Canada, 1977).

Boas, F., *Tsimshian Mythology*, Thirty-First Annual Report for the Bureau of American Ethnology for the years 1909-10 (Washington, DC: Smithsonian Institution, 1916).

Brealey, K., "Travels from Point Ellice: Peter O'Reilly and the Indian Reserve System in British Columbia," *BC Studies*, 115/116 (Autumn/Winter 1997-98): 180-236.

Cail, R. E., *Land, Man and the Law: The Disposal of Crown Lands in British Columbia, 1871-1913* (Vancouver: University of British Columbia, 1974).

Cole, D., and I. Chaikin, *An Iron Hand Upon the People: The Law Against the Potlatch on the Northwest Coast* (Vancouver: Douglas & McIntyre, 1990).

Coutu, P. R., and L. Hoffman-Mercredi, *Ikonze: The Stones of Traditional Knowledge: A History of Northeastern Alberta* (Edmonton: Thunderwoman Ethnographics, 1999).

Cove, J., *Shattered Images: Dialogues and Meditations on Tsimshian Narratives* (Ottawa: Carleton University Press, 1987).

Cove, J., and G. F. MacDonald (Eds.), *Tsimshian Narratives*, vol. I and II, collected by Marius Barbeau and William Beynon (Ottawa: Canadian Museum of Civilization, 1987).

Cumming, P., and N. Mickenberg, *Native Rights in Canada*, 2nd ed. (Toronto: Indian-Eskimo Association of Canada, 1972).

Daly, R., *"Our Box Was Full": Ethnography of the Plaintiffs* (Vancouver: UBC Press, 2004).

Duff, W., "The Fort Victoria Treaties," *BC Studies,* 3 (Fall 1969): 3-57.

Fisher, R., *Contact and Conflict: Indian-European Relations in British Columbia, 1774-1890* (Vancouver: UBC Press, 1977).

_____, "Joseph Trutch and Indian Land Policy," *BC Studies,* 12 (1971-72): 3-33.

Foster, H., "The Queen's Law Is Better than Yours: International Homicide in Early British Columbia," in J. Phillips, T. Loo, and S. Lewthwaite (Eds.), *Essays in the History of Canadian Law,* vol. 5, *Crime and Criminal Justice* (Toronto: University of Toronto Press, 1994), pp. 41-111.

Freedman, R., "The Space for Aboriginal Self-Government in British Columbia: The Effect of the Decision of the British Columbia Court of Appeal in *Delgamuukw* v. *British Columbia,*" *UBC Law Review,* 51 (1994): 28(1).

Galois, R. M., "The History of the Upper Skeena Region, 1850 to 1927," *Native Studies Review,* 9: 2 (1993-94): 113-83.

_____, "The Burning of Kitsegukla, 1872," *BC Studies,* 94 (1992): 59-81.

Galois, R. M., and S. Marsden, "The Tsimshian, The Hudson's Bay Company, and the Geopolitics of the Northwest Coast Fur Trade, 1787-1840," *Canadian Geographer,* 39 (1995): 169-83.

Gluckman, M., *Ideas in Barotse Jurisprudence* (New Haven: Yale University Press, 1965).

Guedon, M.-F., quoted in C. Faber, "Afterwards: Time in a Box," in M. Sequin (Ed.), *Tsimshian: Images of the Past, Views from the Present* (Vancouver: University of British Columbia Press, 1984), p. 309.

Howay, F. W., "An Outline of the Maritime Fur Trade" (Report of the Canadian Historical Association, 1932).

Lowie, R. H., *Primitive Society* (London: Routledge, 1921).

Mackay, C., "The Collins Overland Telegraph," *British Columbia Historical Quarterly,* 10 (July 1946): 187-215.

Mackie, R., "The Colonization of Vancouver Island, 1849-1858," *BC Studies,* 96 (1992/1993): 3 at 4.

McDonald, J. A., *Trying to Make a Life: The Historical Political Economy of the Kitsumalum,* unpublished PhD Diss. (University of British Columbia: Department of Anthropology and Sociology, 1985).

_____, "Images of the Nineteenth Century Economy of the Tsimshian," in M. Sequin (Ed.), *The Tsimshian: Images of the Past, Views of the Present* (Vancouver: UBC Press, 1984), pp. 40-44.

Meilleur, H., *A Pour of Rain: Stories from a West Coast Fort* (Victoria: Sono Nis Press, 1980).

Molloy, T., *The World is Our Witness: The Historic Journey of the Nisga'a into Canada* (Calgary: Fifth House: 2000).

Patterson, P., "A Decade of Change: Origins of the Nishga and Tsimshian Land Protests in the 1880s," *Journal of Canadian Studies*, 18(3) (1983): 40-54.

Pierce, W. H., *From Potlatch to Pulpit: Being the Autobiography of the Rev. William Henry Pierce, Native Missionary to the Indian Tribes of the Northwest Coast of British Columbia* (Vancouver: Vancouver Bindery Ltd., 1933).

Preston, R., *Cree Narrative*, 2nd edition (Montreal: McGill-Queens Press, 2002).

Rasmussen, K., *Iglulik and Caribou Eskimo Texts*, Report of the Fifth Thule Expedition, 1921-1924, vol. 3 (Copenhagen: 1930).

Ray, A. J., "Fur Trade History and the Gitksan-Wet'suwet'en Comprehensive Claim: Men of Property and the Exercise of Title," in K. Abel and J. Friesen (Eds.), *Aboriginal Resource Use in Canada: Historical and Legal Aspects* (Winnipeg: University of Manitoba Press, 1991), p. 301-16.

_____, *The Early Economic History of the Gitksan-Wet'suwet'n-Babine Tribal Territories, 1822-1915* (Gitksan-Wet'suwet'en Tribal Council, 1985)

Ray, A. J., J. Miller and F. Tough, *Bounty and Benevolence: A History of Saskatchewan Treaties* (Montreal: McGill-Queen's University Press, 2000).

Roth, C. F., "Goods, Names, and Selves: Rethinking the Tsimshian Potlatch," *American Ethnologist*, 29(1) (2002): 123-150.

Rushford, S., *Bear Lake Athapaskan Kinship and Task Formation* (Ottawa: National Museum of Man, Mercury Series, 1984).

Sequin, M. (Ed.), *The Tsimshian: Images of the Past, Views from the Present* (Vancouver: UBC Press, 1984).

Slattery, B., "Understanding Aboriginal Rights," Canadian Bar Review, 66 (1987): 727-83.

Speck, F. G., "Penobscot Tales and Religious Beliefs," The Journal of American Folklore, 48 (187) (Jan.-Mar. 1935): 1-107.

Tennant, P., *Aboriginal Peoples and Politics: The Indian Land Question in British Columbia, 1849-1989* (Vancouver: UBC Press, 1990).

Walters, M., "British Imperial Constitutional Law and Aboriginal Rights: A Comment on *Delgamuukw* v. *British Columbia*," *Queen's Law Journal*, 17 (1995): 350.

Wicken, W. C., *Mi'Kmaq Treaties on Trial: History, Land and Donald Marshall Junior* (Toronto: University of Toronto Press, 2001).

Wilson, G., *The Land Rights of Individuals Among the Nyakyusa* (Rhodes-Livingstone Papers, 1938).

Newspaper Articles

"An Eye for an Eye," Victoria *Daily Colonist*, (21 June 1884), n.p.

"Chiefs of Kitseguecla," Victoria *Daily Colonist*, (7 Sept. 1884), n.p.

Dolha, L., "Province Recognizes 'Political Legitimacy'," *Kahtou: The Voice of BC's First Nations*, 10(1) (1992) at 1-2.

Editorial, Victoria *Daily Colonist* (21 June 1884) n.p.

Editorial, Victoria *Daily Colonist* (9 July 1872) n.p.

T. Glavin, "BC Joins Indians, Feds for Land Talks," *Vancouver Sun*, (Mar. 21 1991) B7.

R. Howard, "BC Land Offer to Natives Small: Target of Less than 5 per cent Sharply Soar Expectations in Band's Claim," *Globe and Mail* (18 May 1995) at A1 and A2.

"Indian Unrest," *Province* Vancouver (16 July 1909) n.p.

"Kitwancool Jim," Victoria *Daily Colonist*, (7 Nov. 1888) n.p.

M. McCullough, "Laying Down the Law: The Gitksan Decision Reinforces Government Indian Policy," (1991) 2 (30) *British Columbia Report: The Weekly Newsmagazine*, 6.

W. H. Pierce, "Evils of Indian Witchcraft," *The Western Recorder* (May 1928): 8.

"Playing Some Pre-election Hard Ball: The NDP Suddenly Adopts a Tough Line in Nisgha and Gitksan Treaty Talks" (1996) 7 (24) *British Columbia Report: The Weekly Newsmagazine*, 9.

Addresses and Statements

L. Akacoket, Oct. 1, 1891 for the New Kitsegucka Meeting, Sept. 30, 1891 in: RG 10 vol. 3571 file 126A.

British Columbia, *Response of the Government of British Columbia to the Position Paper of the Nishga Tribal Council*, 10 Jan. 1978.

J. Chrétien, "Statement made by the Honourable Jean Chrétien," Minister of Indian Affairs and Northern Development on Claims of Indian and Inuit People, Aug. 8, 1973

Gitksan-Carrier Declaration, Kispiox, BC, Nov. 7, 1977.

O. Lippert, "Assessing the *Delgam'Uukw* Decision: A Law and Economic Perspective" (Ottawa: The Fraser Institute, 1998) at 11.6.

E. Pettingell, Sept. 18, 1874 in: Church Missionary Society, Duncan Papers 16055.

United Tribes, "Statement of the United Tribes of Northern British Columbia for the Government of Canada," Feb. 27, 1919.

Agreements

British Columbia, Gitksan and Wet'suwet'en, An Accord of Recognition and Respect June 13, 1994.

Canada, Northwest Territories, and The Tlicho, Land Claims and Self-government Agreement among the Tlicho and the Government of the Northwest Territories and Canada.

Gitxsan and British Columbia, "A Cooperative Agreement to Plan and Manage Forest Use" July 2, 1998.

Gitxsan and British Columbia, A Reconciliation Agreement between Her Majesty the Queen in Right of British Columbia and The Hereditary Chiefs of the Gitxsan, Sept. 14, 1998.

Lheidli T'enneh, Canada, and British Columbia, "Lheidli T'enneh Agreement-in-Principle," May 2, 2003.

Quebec, Grand Council of the Crees (of Quebec) and Northern Quebec Inuit Association and Canada, Agreement between the Government of Quebec, Grand Council of the Crees (of Quebec) and Northern Quebec Inuit Association and the Government of Canada (Ottawa: Department of Indian and Northern Affairs, 1975).

Colonial Document Collections

British Columbia, *Further Papers relative to the Affairs of British Columbia, Part III: Copies of Dispatches from the Governor of British Columbia to the Secretary of State for the Colonies, and from the Secretary of State to the Governor, Relative to the Government of the Colony* (London, Eng.: Printers to the Queen, 1860).

British Columbia Legislative Council, *Debate on the Subject of Confederation with Canada, Reprinted from the Government Gazette Extraordinary of Mar., 1870* (Victoria, BC: Queen's Printer, 1870).

British Columbia, *Papers Connected to the Indian Land Question, 1850 to 1875* (Victoria, BC: Queens Printer, 1875).

British Columbia, "Papers Relating to the Colonization of Vancouver Island," in: *Report of the Provincial Archives Department of British Columbia*, British Columbia Sessional Papers (Victoria, BC: King's Printer, 1914) at V 72 and V 73.

Canada, Annual Report of the Department of Indian Affairs, 1885, Sessional Papers, vol. 19(4) (49 Victoria) (Ottawa: Department of Indian Affairs, 1886) n.p.

W. E. Hodgins, comp. Correspondence, reports of the Ministers of Justice and Order in Council upon the Subject of Dominion and Provincial Legislation, 1867-1920 (Ottawa, Ont: Government Printing Bureau, 1896-1922).

J. Pope, *Correspondence of Sir John Macdonald: Selections from the Correspondence of Sir John Alexander Macdonald, G.C.B., First Prime Minister of Canada* (Toronto: Oxford University Press, 1921).

Letters and Journal Entries

A. Barclay, 17 Dec. 1849, Winnipeg, Man.: Provincial Archives of Manitoba and Hudson's Bay Archives at A.6/28 folio: 90d-92.

J. Cashore to D. Ryan, 1 Feb. 1996, Victoria, BC: Ministry of Aboriginal Affairs File No. 63300-20/Gitx/COR, 1996.

N. Fitzstubbs to C.W.D. Clifford in: RG10 vol. 3628 file 6244-1.

N. Fitzstubbs to Attorney General, 5 Jan. 1889, in Babine Agency Letter-book RG 10 vol. 1585.

T. Hankin to Lieutenant Governor J. Trutch, "Petition of Indians at Kitesgoually to Lieutenant Governor," National Archives Canada, National Archives of Canada,

RG 10 volume 1159.

A. W. Humphrey, Diary 7 June 1874, British Columbia Archives and Records Service E/C/H 881.

Rev. D. Jennings Port Wessington, BC, 11 Jan. 1893, in The Missionary Outlook, (Spring) 1893.

R. E. Loring to A.W. Vowell, 15 July 1897, in Babine Agency Letter-book RG 10 1585.

J. McDougall to McLean, 21 Sept. 1909, in RG 10, vol. 7786, file 27151-1.

J. McDougall to Oliver, 22 Sept. 1910, in RG 10, vol. 4020, file 280 at 470-72.

I. Powell, P. O'Reilly, G. Vernon to Chief Isadore and the Kootenay Indians 10 Oct. 1887, in Canada, British Columbia, *Reserve Allocation Commission Annual Report, 1887*.

C. M. Tate, Circular Letter, 16 Dec. 1912, in RG 10, vol. 11023 file 662.

Rev. Robert Tomlinson, Journal, 1874, Church Missionary Society, University of British Columbia Library, vol. 106 #143.

J. W. Trutch to W. Moberly, 10 Oct. 1865, GR 1372 (Reel: B-1351).

Memoranda of Understandings and Policies

British Columbia, *Response of the Government of British Columbia to the Position Paper of the Nishga Tribal Council*, 10 Jan. 1978.

Canada, Discussion Paper on Indian Land Claims in BC (Department of Indian and Northern Affairs for the Conference on Aboriginal Rights, Prince George, Sept. 22 to 24, 1978).

Canada, *Statement of the Government of Canada on Indian Policy, 1969* (Ottawa: Department of Indian Affairs, 1969).

Canada and British Columbia, *Memorandum of Understanding of the Province of British Columbia and Canada Respecting the Sharing of Pre-treaty Costs, Settlement Costs, Implementation Costs and the Cost of Self-government*, 1993.

Department of Indian Affairs and Northern Development, *In All Fairness: A Native Claims Policy, Comprehensive Claims* (Ottawa: Ministry of Supply and Services, 1981).

Department of Indian Affairs and Northern Development, *Outstanding Business: A Native Claims Policy, Specific Claims* (Ottawa: Ministry of Supply and Services,

1982).

Gitksan-Carrier Declaration, Kispiox, BC, Nov. 7, 1977.

Gitxsan, *"Substantive Issues, Draft Three,"* 15 Jan. 1996 (Hazelton, BC: Gitxsan Hereditary Chiefs Office, 1996).

Reports

British Columbia Gazette, 1907.

Canada, Annual Report Department of Indian Affairs, 1889.

Canada, R*eport of the Commission on North West Indians Sessional Papers, 1888.*

Canada, Houses of Parliament, Senate, Special Joint Committee of the Senate and House of Commons Appointed to Inquire into the Claims of the Allied tribes of British Columbia, as set forth by their Petition submitted to Parliament in 1927, *Report and Evidence*, Appendix to the Journal of the Senate of Canada, First Session of the Sixteenth Parliament, 1926 – 1927. (Ottawa: King's Printer, 1927).

Canada, British Columbia, *Reserve Allocation Commission Annual Report, 1887.*

R. Daly, *"Our Box Was Full": The Gitksan-Wet'suwet'en Economy"* Opinion Evidence, June 1987.

Department of Fisheries and Oceans, *Strengthening Our Relationship: Aboriginal Fisheries Strategy and Beyond* (Ottawa: Department of Fisheries and Oceans, www.dfo-mpo.gc.ca/cummunic/afs/afsoct03__e.htm).

Canada, *Northern Frontier, Northern Homeland: The Report of the Mackenzie Valley Pipeline Inquiry, 1977.*

H. B. Hawthorne (Ed.), A Survey of the Contemporary Indians of Canada: A Report on Economic, Political, Educational Needs and Policies, vol. 1 (Ottawa: Indian Affairs Branch, 1966).

W. J. McKay, "Report of the Kamloops Agency," in Canada, Annual Report of the Department of Indian Affairs, 1885, Sessional Papers, vol. 19(4) (49 Victoria) (Ottawa: Department of Indian Affairs, 1886) n.p.

R. Michell, "The Gitksan-Wet'suwet'en Blanket Trapline Proposal," submitted to the Department of Fish and Wildlife, (Feb. 19, 1985, Hagwiiget, BC).

A. Robinson, *Fact Finder's Report on the Suspension of the Gitxsan Treaty Negotiations* (Vancouver, BC: British Columbia Treaty Commission, 1996).

Statutes

An Act to Amend "The Indian Act, 1880" S.C. 1884, c.27 (47 Vict.).

An Act for conferring certain privileges on the more Advanced Bands of the Indians of Canada S.C. (47 Vict. c. 27 1884).

An Act to Amend the Indian Act, S.C. (1926 – 1927) c. 32 (17 Geo. V).

British Columbia Treaty Commission Act, 1995 c.45.

Canadian Charter of Rights and Freedoms, Part I of the Consititution Act, 1982, Appendix II.

Constitution Act, Sched. B of the Canada Act (U.K.), 1982 c. 11.

Indian Act R.S.C. 1985 c. 1-5

Indian Oil and Gas Act, (R.S.C. 1985 c. 1 – 7)

Treaty Commission Act RSBC 1996 c. 461

Treaties

Canada and The Committee for Original People's Entitlement, The Western Arctic Claim: The Inuvialuit Final Agreement (Ottawa: The Department of Indian and Northern Affairs, 1985).

Canada and the Tungavik Inuit of Nunavut, Agreement between the Inuit of the Nunavut Settlement Area and Her Majesty the Queen in Right of Canada (Ottawa: Department of Indian Affairs and Northern Development, 1993).

Canada, British Columbia and Nisga'a Nation, Nisga'a Final Agreement (Ottawa: Department of Indian and Northern Affairs, 1999).

Great Britain, *Treaty between Her Majesty and the United States of America, for the settlement of the Oregon Boundary*, signed Washington, 15 June, 1846.

Quebec, Grand Council of the Crees (of Quebec) and Northern Quebec Inuit Association and Canada, Agreement between the Government of Quebec, Grand Council of the Crees (of Quebec) and Northern Quebec Inuit Association and the Government of Canada (Ottawa: Department of Indian and Northern Affairs, 1975).

Cases

Calder v. *the Attorney General of British Columbia* [1973] S.C.R. 313.

Delgam'Uukw (Muldoe) et al. v. *R. in Right of British Columbia and Attorney General of Canada* [1991] 3 W.W.R. 97.

Delgam'Uukw (Muldoe) et al. v. *R. in Right of British Columbia and Attorney General of Canada* [1993] 5 W.W.R. 97.

Delgam'Uukw (Muldoe) et al. v. *R. in Right of British Columbia and Attorney General of Canada* [1997] 3 S.C.R. 1010.

Guerin v. *the Queen* [1984] 2 S.C.R. 335.

Haida Nation v. *British Columbia (Minister of Forests)*, [2004] S.C.R. 511.

Hamlet of Baker Lake (et al.) v. *Minister of Indian Affairs and Northern Development (et al.)* (1979), 107 D.L.R. (3rd) 513.

La societé de développment de la Baie James, [1975] R.J.Q. 166.

Mikisew Cree First Nation v. *Canada (Minister of Canadian Heritage)*, [2005] 3 S.C.R. 388

R. v. *Sparrow* [1990] *1 S.C.R. 1075.*

R. v. *Van der Peet* [1996] *2 S.R.C. 507.*

Re Paulette et al. and Registrar of Titles (No 2) [1973] 6 W.W.R. 97.

Taku River Tlingit First Nation v. *British Columbia (Project Assessment Director)* [2004] S.C.R. 550.

Uukw et al v. *R. in Right of British Columbia and the Attorney General of Canada* [1988] 1 C.N.L.R. 173.

Proceedings

Canada and British Columbia, *Royal Commission on Indian Affairs for the Province of British Columbia*, "Meeting with the Kuldoe Band or Tribe of Indians at Hazelton on Tuesday July 13, 1915."

M. Brown, Commissioned Evidence (1985) vol. 1 Sept. 18. (1)

_____, Commissioned Evidence (1985) vol. 2 Sept. 19. (1)

_____, Commissioned Evidence (1985) vol. 3 Sept. 21. (1)

_____, Commissioned Evidence (1986) vol. 4 Jan. 22. (65)

R. Daly, Proceedings at Trial, (1989) vol. 187 Feb. 23.

N. Fitzstubbs, Proceedings at Hazelton, (1888) Oct. 18 in: RG 10 vol. 3802 file 49774.

R. Galois, Proceedings at Trial, (1989) vol. 226 May 18. (16450)

_____, Proceedings at Trial, (1989) vol. 227 May 19. (16553)

House of Assembly, Jan. 28, 1860 in: British *Colonist* (29 Jan. 1861).

F. Johnson, Commissioned Evidence, (1986) vol. 1 Sept. 2. (1)

M. Johnson, The *Adawaak* of *Tsibasaa* and *Antgulilbix*, Proceedings at Trial (1987) vol. 11 May 27 at 665-68.

_____, Proceedings at Trial, (1987) vol. 13 May 29. (784)

A. Joseph, Proceedings at Trial, (1987) vol. 2 May 11. (65)

M. McKenzie, Proceedings at Trial, (1987) vol. 3 May 13. (142)

_____, Proceedings at Trial, (1987) vol. 4 May 14. (207)

_____, Proceedings at Trial, (1987) vol. 5 May 15 (281)

_____, Proceedings at Trial, (1987) vol. 6 May 19. (338)

_____, Proceedings at Trial, (1987) vol. 7 May 20. (383)

_____, Proceedings at Trial, (1987) vol. 8 May 21. (439)

_____, Proceedings at Trial, (1987) vol. 10 May 26. (560)

S. Marsden, Proceedings at Trial, (1988) vol. 92 May 5. (5820)

_____, Proceedings at Trial, (1988) vol. 93 May 6. (5891)

_____, Proceedings at Trial, (1988) vol. 94 May 9. (5932)

_____, Proceedings at Trial, (1989) vol. 232 June 5. (16931)

A. Mathews, Proceedings at Trial, (1988) vol. 73 Mar. 14. (4513)

_____, Proceedings at Trail, (1988) vol. 74 Mar. 15. (4586)

_____, Proceedings at Trial, (1988) vol. 75 Mar. 16. (4661)

_____, Proceedings at Trial, (1988) vol. 76 Mar. 17. (4691)

_____, Proceedings at Trial, (1988) vol. 77 Mar. 18. (4759)

J. Morrison, Proceedings at Trial, (1988) vol. 82 Apr. 18. (5081)

_____, Proceedings at Trial, (1988) vol. 83 Apr. 19. (5163)

_____, Proceedings at Trial, (1988) vol. 84 Apr. 20. (5247)

K. Muldoe, Proceedings at Trial, (1987) vol. 2 May 11. (65)

P. Muldoe, Proceedings at Trial, (1988) vol. 97 May 16. (6084)

_____, Proceedings at Trial, (1988) vol. 100 May 19. (6297)

_____, Proceedings at Trial, (1988) vol. 103 May 25. (6462)

Proceedings, New Kitseguckla Meeting (1891) Sept. 30.

A. Ray, Proceedings at Trial, (1988) vol. 203 Mar. 21. (13410)

S. Rush, Proceedings at Trial, (1987) vol. 2 May 11. (65)

J. Ryan, Proceedings at Trial, (1988) vol. 79 Mar. 23. (4975)

_____, Proceedings at Trial, (1988) vol. 80 Mar. 23. (4996)

O. Ryan, Proceedings at Trial, (1987) vol. 16 June 10. (1003)

_____, Proceedings at Trial, (1987) vol. 17 June 11. (1076)

_____, Proceedings at Trial, (1987) vol. 19 June 15. (1217)

V. Smith, Proceedings at Trial, (1988) vol. 89 May 2. (5614)

G. Williams, Proceedings at Trial, (1988) vol. 105 May 30. (6620)

_____, Proceedings at Trial, (1988) vol. 106 May 31. (6687)

_____, Proceedings at Trial, (1988) vol. 107 June 1. (6761)

S. Williams, Commissioned Evidence (1988) vol. 1 Apr. 11. (1)

_____, Commissioned Evidence (1988) vol. 2 Apr. 18. (140)

Index

A

Aboriginal Aquatic Resource and Ocean Management Program 138

Aboriginal self government 44, 51, 56, 57, 61, 62, 64, 73-6, 77-80, 82-3, 126, 129, 130, 133-4, 146-7

Aboriginal title 39, 45-6, 48, 49, 50-1, 53-4, 56-7, 65-6, 80-3, 128-30; to be ceded 11, 24-5, 27, 54, 57-61, 83-4, 125, 127, 135-6; considered *sui generis* 25, 73, 78; Crown denial of 25, 42, 59; current Supreme Court perspective on 24-5, 27, 73-4, 82, 83-4, 125; extinguishment of 24, 44, 51, 56, 59-60, 82, 66-7, 73-4, 79, 81-3, 125-6, 127, 128, 136, 145

Acts of Reconciliation 24, 134-7

adawaak (*wilp's* historical narrative) 29, 56, 57, 65, 68-70, 86, 93, 108-11, 115, 120, 123; importance of 25-6, 70, 85, 87, 90-2, 95, 96, 124

am bilan (ceremonial aprons) 85, 92, 102

'am halitx (headdresses) 85, 92

amnigwootxw (permission to access or use a territory: privileged reciprocity) granted to Canada 24, 135; interpreted in *Delgam'Uukw* 71-2; principles of as basis for society 99-102, 106-7, 120, 134-6, 140

Andemane (Skeena territorial boundary) 47

Anhluult'ukwsim Laxmihl Angwinga'asan Nisga'a (Nisga'a Memorial Lava Bed Provincial Park) 130

andimbanak (spouse's kinship group) 94, 98

anjok (asking permission) 99

An si bilaa 104

Antgulilbix Xsgooim 104

An t'ookxw, the "Banquet Table" 102

assimilation 38, 40, 41, 69

Patricia Dawn Mills grew up around the Beaver and
Slavey people in Northern Alberta, and now lives in
Vancouver with her husband and daughter. She holds
a PhD in Native Law, History, and Anthropology
from the University of British Columbia Faculty of
Law. Her research includes the intersection of First
Nations and Canadian state property rights,
especially in the area of mineral, oil, and gas
development. Currently, Dr. Mills holds an adjunct
position at the Norman B. Keevil Institute of Mining
Engineering at the University of British Columbia.